Lee Canter's

BACK TO SCHOOL WITH ASSERTIVE DISCIPLINE®

A Publication of Canter & Associates

Staff Writers
Patricia Ryan Sarka
Marcia Shank

Contributing Writer
Bob Winberry

Illustrators
Patricia Briles
Jane Yamada

Design & Photos
The Arcane Corporation

Editorial Staff
Marlene Canter
Carol Provisor
Kathy Winberry

© 1990 Canter & Associates
P.O. Box 2113, Santa Monica, CA 90407-2113
800-262-4347   310-395-3221
www.canter.net

ISBN #0-939007-31-2

Printed in the United States of America
First printing April 1990
04 03 02 01 00   14 13 12 11 10

PD4158

CONTENTS

ABOUT ASSERTIVE DISCIPLINE®

A classroom in which teachers can teach and students can learn is the environment desired by educators everywhere. Lee Canter's Assertive Discipline enables you to achieve that environment through a positive, skill-based approach to classroom management—a system of rules and consequences, balanced with rewards for appropriate behavior *plus* specialized techniques designed to address the most difficult behavior management problems. Assertive Discipline can help you deal successfully with every kind of disruption at every grade level.

Assertive Discipline can help you

- improve discipline in your classroom.
- create a positive environment for all students.
- involve parents in your educational program.
- keep students motivated and learning.

From textbooks, posters and activity books to planbooks and motivating workbooks—Lee Canter & Associates offers a complete line of comprehensive, easy-to-use materials designed to help you define, implement and accomplish your goals.

INTRODUCTION
Back to School with Assertive Discipline

You can't teach—and your students can't learn—when discipline problems disrupt your classroom. You need to plan *now*, before school begins, to create an environment that will ensure a successful school year for everyone. The goal of *Back to School with Assertive Discipline* is to give you a sequence of steps you can take that will allow you to start the school year with a new attitude of confidence—an attitude that comes from knowing you're well-prepared to deal with any situation that arises in the upcoming year.

How to Use this Book:

Back to School with Assertive Discipline is divided into eight content parts. Work through the book sequentially. Each part gives you step-by-step instructions for achieving specific goals. As you begin to build your back-to-school repertoire of techniques, reproducibles, classroom visual aids, organizational ideas, motivators and more, you will soon see a successful year unfolding before you!

Here's what you'll find inside:

Part 1—Your Assertive Discipline Plan
The foundation of a smoothly running classroom is an Assertive Discipline Plan that clearly states the rules of the classroom, consequences for students who choose not to observe the rules, and positive reinforcement for students who behave appropriately. Part 1 will give you the guidelines, posters and worksheets you need to put together a discipline plan that works for you *and* your students.

Part 2—Planning to Teach Specific Directions

Effective behavior management means that students know how to behave in *all* situations. Therefore, it is important—at the start of the school year—to teach students directions for all classroom activities. Plan your "following directions" lessons now. Our easy-to-follow guidelines and open-ended lesson plan make it easy.

Part 3—Classroom Organization

A well-organized classroom can help you avoid many discipline problems. Will students' desks be arranged in a manner that is conducive to learning? Will your desk be well-stocked with necessary items? Will materials be clearly marked and easily available to students? Get organized now and save time and annoying disruptions later

Part 4—Back-to-School Bulletin Boards

Welcome your students back to school with a bright, exciting environment that's more than just something to look at! Our back-to-school bulletin boards will help you manage student behavior, display important classroom information, exhibit appropriately done assignments and more! Reproducible masters provide appealing artwork that will grab your students' attention.

Part 5—Getting Parents on Your Side

Don't wait until parent conference time to initiate contact with parents. Take action *now* to plan to get parents involved in your educational program right at the start of the school year. Reproducible "welcome back" notes, Parent Handbook suggestions, Back-to-School Night invitations, parent volunteer notes (and more) will go a long way toward gaining the attention of parents

Part 6—Planning for Homework

A successful homework program begins with a homework policy. In Part 6 you will find guidelines for writing your own homework policy plus lesson ideas to help you teach students the skills they need to complete homework assignments appropriately. Reproducible take-home posters will help students set up a proper study area at home.Special homework awards will help you motivate students to do their best work.

Part 7—Final Preparations

Are you ready? Here are some first-day-of-school activity suggestions that will help you and your students get acquainted and start off on a productive new year.

Part 8—Back to School!

Now it's time to reap the rewards of all your planning. You are prepared, confident, and ready to walk into your classroom with an assertive, take-charge attitude. Part 8 contains some extra reminders and suggestions to help guide you through the first important days.

Reproducibles

Back to School with Assertive Discipline contains over 75 reproducible masters. These reproducibles are located in the Appendix at the back of the book. Each reproducible is introduced within the text portion of the book. Suggestions for use are given as well as any necessary preparation instructions.

BEFORE YOU BEGIN

You are about to be introduced to techniques that will help you embark on a productive school year. As you proceed through this book, keep in mind that one of the keys to the successful implementation of these techniques is the assertiveness and confidence you project as you interact with students and parents.

Assertive teachers share these characteristics:

- They get their needs met.
- They clearly and firmly communicate.
- They will not tolerate inappropriate student behavior, students stopping them from teaching or stopping someone else from learning.
- They back up their words with actions.

When teachers are assertive, and clearly and firmly communicate their wants and feelings to students, they send a very clear message: "I will not tolerate any student stopping me from teaching or others from learning."

By being assertive, teachers communicate what they expect from students, and what students can expect in return from the teacher. Assertive teachers set firm, consistent limits, while at the same time remain aware of the students' need for warmth and support.

Throughout this book we have included a variety of Assertive Discipline Teacher Tips. By integrating these tips into your own teaching style, you will develop and maintain the assertive attitude that demonstrates your professionalism to students and parents alike.

YOUR ASSERTIVE DISCIPLINE PLAN

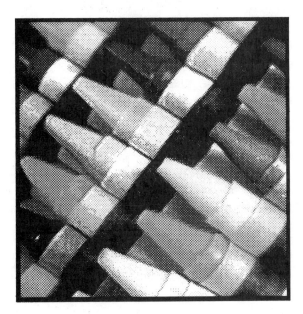

Color your classroom with confidence—a bright new year is awaiting! Everyone gets to begin again. You included. Are you looking forward to the months ahead, or are you facing them with something less than enthusiasm? Chances are, if it's the latter, the reason has something to do with discipline.

Take a minute now to list three of the most troublesome discipline problems that affected your classroom last year.

1 _____

2 _____

3 _____

That's what Part 1 of this book is all about—making sure these problems don't interfere with your teaching goals again. Together, we're going to remedy what went wrong last year and prepare for an even better year to come.

INTRODUCING THE ASSERTIVE DISCIPLINE PLAN

Establish this plan and you'll take an important step toward a productive new year.

The Reason
An Assertive Discipline Plan is a system that allows you to clarify what behaviors you expect of students and what they can expect from you in return.

The Goal
To have a fair and consistent way in which to deal with all students who misbehave, thereby creating an atmosphere conducive to teaching and allowing more time on-task for learning.

An Assertive Discipline Plan consists of three parts:

RULES
that students must follow at all times.

CONSEQUENCES
that students receive when they choose not to follow the rules.

REWARDS
for students who follow the rules.

On the following pages you will be developing your own Assertive Discipline Plan. You'll start off by establishing classroom rules and work your way through determining consequences and rewards. When you are finished, you will have a discipline plan designed to meet your own specific needs—and the needs of your students.

RULES

You know that you want your students to behave in class. But you can't expect them to behave according to your standards if they don't know what those standards are. Remember, each child walking through your door is bringing a set of behaviors learned in other classrooms, at home or from friends. These behaviors may or may not be appropriate *or* compatible with your teaching style. In any case, you need to get all of your students on *your* behavior track. Students need to know exactly what is expected of them. That's why good classroom management—and your Assertive Discipline Plan—begins with clearly defined rules or expectations.

Your Assertive Discipline Plan will contain no more than five rules. These are the general rules that must be in effect at all times. These rules will be the foundation upon which you will manage behavior in the classroom.

Guidelines for Developing Classroom Rules

- Your first classroom rule should be "Follow directions the first time they are given."

- Make sure that your rules are observable. Rules such as "Be good" are too vague and not observable. Rules such as "Raise your hand and wait to be called upon before you speak" are observable.

- Make sure your rules are in the students' best interest. For instance, having a rule that requires first-graders to remain in their seats all day is not reasonable nor is it in the students' best interest.

- Rules should be stated as a positive rather than a negative whenever possible: "Keep hands to yourself," rather than "No hitting your neighbor."

- The rules you choose should address those behaviors that are most important to you and your teaching style.

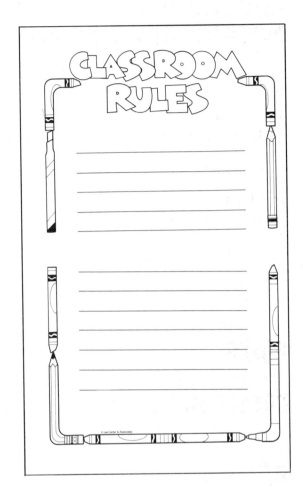

Here are some examples of rules that have proven successful in classrooms:

Primary
Kindergarten through Third Grade

• Follow directions the first time they are given.

• Keep hands, feet and objects to yourself.

• Do not leave the room without permission.

Intermediate
Fourth through Sixth Grade

• Follow directions the first time they are given.

• Keep hands, feet and objects to yourself.

• Have all materials and supplies at your desk and be ready to begin working when the bell rings.

• Do not swear or tease.

Take time now to look ahead and decide upon the most important behaviors you will require of your students. In the spaces below write your list of classroom rules. Remember that these rules, when broken, will always carry a consequence. It is important, therefore to carefully think through each rule you choose.

1 _____

2 _____

3 _____

4 _____

5 _____

See the reproducible Rules Poster (Appendix pages 98-99)

CONSEQUENCES

Students need to be taught to be responsible for their actions. They need to realize that the choice is theirs: to follow the rules of the classroom and enjoy the rewards or to disregard the rules and accept the consequences. Your Assertive Discipline Plan lets you take the guesswork out of disciplinary action by being prepared *before* behavior problems arise.

Guidelines for Choosing Disciplinary Consequences

- Make sure the consequences are something you are comfortable using. For example, don't keep students after school as a consequence if you are not comfortable staying after school.

- Students should not like the consequences, but under no circumstances should they be physically or psychologically harmful to the students.

- Organize your consequences into a discipline hierarchy. The hierarchy contains a maximum of five consequences listed in order of severity.

- Consequences should include calling parents and sending students to the principal, if appropriate. Parent and principal contact should always be included towards the end of the hierarchy.

- The discipline hierarchy should also include a severe clause to be utilized *immediately* if a student fights or refuses to do what he or she is told, etc. The severe clause may be, for example, sending the student to the principal.

- The consequences should comply with school and district policy.

Examples of Disciplinary Consequences
Warning (always first)
Time out away from group
Recess detention
After-school detention
In-class detention
Letter to parents
Phone call to parents
Send to another teacher's room
Send to principal

Here is a typical discipline hierarchy for the elementary grades:

First time a student breaks a rule
Warning

Second time a student breaks a rule
5 minutes working away from the group

Third time a student breaks a rule
10 minutes working away from the group

Fourth time a student breaks a rule
Call parents

Fifth time a student breaks a rule
Send to principal

SEVERE CLAUSE
Send to principal

Now list the disciplinary consequences you will use in your classroom this year. Remember: It is not the severity but the inevitability of receiving the consequence that has impact.

First time student breaks a rule:

_____

Second time student breaks a rule:

_____

Third time student breaks a rule:

_____

Fourth time student breaks a rule:

_____

Fifth time student breaks a rule:

_____

SEVERE CLAUSE

_____

See the reproducible Consequences Poster (Appendix page 100).

REWARDS

Negative consequences will stop unwanted behavior. But only positive consequences will *change* behavior. And that's the result you are after. To get that result, you must make every effort to focus on the positive behavior of your students—not the negative behavior. Positive responses to expected behavior should become a natural, consistent part of your teaching style.

Your positive reinforcement system, therefore, is the core of your Assertive Discipline Plan. It is the single most important tool you have to help students shape appropriate behaviors. You need to "catch your students being good" and take every opportunity to let them know that you notice and appreciate their efforts.

Have fun with positives! Positive reinforcement should be enjoyable for you as well as for your students. Read the guidelines for positive reinforcement on this page. Then take a look on pages 14 and 15 for ideas of both individual and classwide positives. Plan to use a variety of approaches. A positive reinforcement system should always be varied and fresh.

Guidelines for Positive Reinforcement

- Use positive reinforcement that you are comfortable with (for example, praising a student for appropriate behavior instead of giving him or her candy).

- The reinforcement should be something the students want and enjoy.

- The reinforcement should be given as soon as the positive behavior is exhibited. (With older students, rewards can be delayed.)

- Use verbal praise frequently.

- Plan ahead of time which specific appropriate behaviors merit reinforcement.

Positives for Individual Students

Reproducibles for the positives on this page can be found in the Appendix on the pages indicated.

a. Positive Notes to Students   (page 102)
Individual awards are an excellent way to let a student know that you've noticed his or her good behavior. Keep these handy. Plan to award a specific number each day.

b. Positive Notes to Parents   (page 103)
Recognize your students' good-behavior efforts by sending home Positive Notes to Parents. This type of praise is very powerful because parents tend to reinforce the praise—and both parent and students appreciate it so much.

c. Desktop Behavior Charts   (page 104)
These Desktop Behavior Charts allow you to stamp (or add a sticker to) a student's chart when he or she follows a predetermined rule. These charts should be taped to each student's desk or kept in a special folder. When the entire chart is filled in, the student receives a reward and the chart is taken home to show parents.

d. Good-Behavior Bonuses   (page 105)
Your positive reinforcement should be varied and fun! Use these Good Behavior Bonuses as special treats for students who follow the rules.

e. You Earned It! Coupons   (page 106)
Keep an ample supply of these redeemable reinforcement coupons on hand at all times. Don't hesitate to award them to deserving students.

f. Best-Behavior Desk Sign   (page 107)
Each day acknowledge a student who has been following the rules of your classroom. The honored student keeps the Best-Behavior Desk Sign on his or her desk and is awarded a special reward (such as choosing the PE game).

a

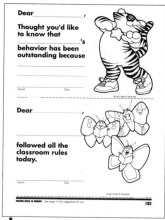

b

c

d

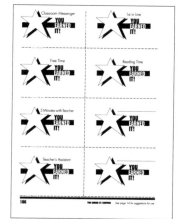

e

f

Positives for the Entire Class

If you want to change or reinforce a behavior for the entire class (or for a number of students) an effective technique is to get them working toward a common goal.

Set up the contingency that when the entire class earns a predetermined number of points for specific good behavior, they will receive a special reward. Whenever the whole class is exhibiting that behavior (for example, quietly entering the classroom after recess) a point is earned.

Many elementary teachers use marbles in a jar to keep track of classwide positive points. Just the sound of a marble dropping into the jar tells the students that they are behaving appropriately. Also, the students can watch the marbles accumulate in the jar and chart their progress toward a reward. Other teachers keep track of points on the chalkboard, or with stickers on a bulletin board. (See page 43 for a classwide positive behavior bulletin board idea.)

Here are some ideas for rewards the entire class can enjoy:

- Free time in class
- Time in class to do homework
- Popcorn while watching a film
- Special arts and crafts projects
- Play radio in class
- Extra P.E. time
- Special lunch or dessert
- Conduct class on the lawn
- Cook in class

Verbal praise is high praise indeed!

The most effective positive reinforcer you can use is verbal praise. When praising students, be very specific and mention the exact behavior you like. Non-specific praise such as, "You did a good job today," is too vague. A comment like "Thank you for getting to work so quickly" lets a student know that you really noticed the good effort being made. Try to praise every student every day!

In the spaces below, write down several individual and classwide positive reinforcements you will use in your classroom this year.

Positive Reinforcements for Individual Students

_____

_____

_____

_____

_____

_____

Positive Reinforcements for the Entire Class

_____

_____

_____

_____

_____

_____

See the reproducible Rewards Poster (Appendix page 101).

YOUR DISCIPLINE PLAN SUPPORT TEAM

You know that you succeed best at your job when you have the support and cooperation of others who are involved in your students' education. This teamwork is especially important in the area of discipline. Make every effort to get the support you need and deserve. Plan some "before-school-begins" tactics that will get parents, administrators, and substitute teachers on your side.

Parent Support

Parent contact is an important part of your discipline plan hierarchy. Make parents aware of your program early in the school year. Enlist their support right away! Then, when a problem arises you are in a position to contact the parents immediately.

The first day of school send home a letter outlining your Assertive Discipline Plan. (See the reproducible letter to parents on Appendix page 108.) Have parents sign the letter and return the signature portion to you.

Your letter should include the following points:

- Correlation of a strong discipline plan to the best possible environment for learning.

- A list of the rules, and positive and negatives consequences of your discipline plan.

- A message enlisting parent support for the plan.

- An invitation to parents to call you with any discipline concerns they might wish to discuss. Include the school and/or your home phone number.

- Parent signature and comment sheet.

NOTE: Communicating your Assertive Discipline Plan to parents is only part of the parent involvement program you need to develop for your classroom. Part 5 will give you many more ideas for getting—and keeping—parents on your side!

Dear Parent,

I am delighted that _____ is in my class this year. We can all look forward to many exciting and rewarding experiences as the year progresses.

As I firmly believe that life-long success depends on self-discipline, I have developed a Classroom Discipline Plan that gives every student the opportunity to manage his or her own behavior. Your child deserves the most positive educational climate possible for academic growth. Therefore, this plan will be in effect at all times.

Classroom Rules

1 _____
2 _____
3 _____
4 _____
5 _____

To encourage students to follow the classroom rules, I reinforce appropriate behavior with

_____

If a student chooses to break a rule, these are the consequences:

| 1st time |
| 2nd time |
| 3rd time |
| 4th time |
| 5th time |
| Severe Disruption |

I have discussed the Classroom Discipline Plan with my students, but I would appreciate it if you would also review the plan with your child, then sign and return the form below. I will be communicating with you frequently throughout the year to keep you aware of your child's progress. Please feel free to contact me at any time.

Teacher's Signature _____ Room Number _____ Date _____

- -

I have read your Classroom Discipline Plan and discussed it with my child.

Parent/Guardian Signature _____ Child's Name _____ Date _____

- -

108   DISCIPLINE PLAN LETTER TO PARENTS See page 17 for suggestions for use.

Administrator Support

You need to know that you have the backing of your administrator—that he or she will support you as you implement your discipline plan. Present your discipline plan to your administrator before school begins. Make sure that you and your administrator are clear about his or her role in your discipline plan. If you have certain expectations of what will take place when you send a student to the principal, make them known now.

Use the Discipline Plan Worksheet (page 109) to help you prepare and present your discipline plan.

Substitute Support

You can't always be there every day. But you can make sure that your classroom continues to run smoothly and productively—no matter who is in charge. To ensure consistent discipline in your classroom, even when you are not present, prepare a discipline plan for substitutes. Fill in your discipline plan on the Substitute Sheet on page 110. Make sure that a copy is left in the office. Put another copy in your lesson plan book or tape it to the top of your desk.

Also: The rules of your classroom must be in effect at all times. Therefore, it is important that any paraprofessionals or volunteers who work in your room understand the Assertive Discipline Plan and the role they are to play in its implementation. Take time to explain the plan to your support staff. Make it very clear how they are to deal with both positive and negative behavior.

DISCIPLINE PLAN WORKSHEET

Teacher ___ Grade ___ Room ___

Rules—Behavior Rules for My Classroom
1 ___
2 ___
3 ___
4 ___
5 ___

Consequences—When a Student Breaks a Rule
1st time ___
2nd time ___
3rd time ___
4th time ___
5th time ___
Severe Clause ___

Rewards—Positives I Will Use When My Students Behave
___

Principal's Comments ___

DISCIPLINE PLAN WORKSHEET *See page 18 for suggestions for use*   **109**

SUBSTITUTE'S PLAN

From the desk of: ___

Dear Substitute:

The following are the guidelines for the Discipline Plan used in my classroom. Please follow them exactly, and leave me a list of students who break the rules and a list of students who behave properly. Thanks.

Classroom Rules
1 ___
2 ___
3 ___
4 ___
5 ___

Consequences
When a student breaks a rule:
1st time ___
2nd time ___
3rd time ___
4th time ___
5th time ___
Severe Clause: If a student exhibits severe misbehavior such as fighting, open defiance, or vulgar language, the following consequence is to be immediately imposed:

Students who behave will be rewarded when I return with:

I appreciate your cooperation in following my Discipline Plan.
Sincerely,

110   SUBSTITUTE SHEET *See page 18 for suggestions for use*

POST YOUR PLAN

You will be introducing your discipline plan to students as soon as school begins (see page 20 for implementation guidelines). Strengthen your message by including "discipline plan" posters as a permanent part of your classroom decor. Posters have been provided for you on pages 98-101 of the Appendix. Write your rules, consequences and rewards on these posters. Display them in a prominent location in your classroom.

Note: You may wish to reproduce the posters on heavy paper, then laminate. As the year progresses you can change your consequences as needed and vary your rewards to keep students motivated.

Congratulations!

You've written your Assertive Discipline Plan. You've just taken the first big step toward improving student behavior in your classroom. And that's a great start. Now step back and take a look at your posters. You can almost see the students cooperating!

ASSERTIVE DISCIPLINE IN ACTION
Implementing Your Assertive Discipline Plan

Introduce the Assertive Discipline Plan to Students

- The first day of school, tell students that the purpose of the plan is to have a fair way of dealing with any behavior situations that arise in class. Explain that the plan consists of three parts:

Rules students are expected to follow at all times.

Consequences students will receive when they choose not to follow the rules.

Rewards students can expect for appropriate behavior.

Implementing Consequences

- Every time a student breaks one of your rules, provide him or her with a disciplinary consequence. Consistency is vital!

- Provide the consequence immediately after the student misbehaves.

- Stay calm when disciplining a student.

- Make sure students know the consequences they will choose for their misbehavior.

- Start each day with a clean slate. Consequences should not be cumulative day to day. They are, however, cumulative throughout the day.

- If your disciplinary consequences do not work, try "tougher" ones. But make sure that any changes are posted and students are informed of these changes.

Implementing Positive Reinforcement

- Rewards should never be taken away as punishment.

- As with disciplinary consequences, students should be aware of your positive reinforcement, awards and activites and how they can earn them.

- Plan ahead of time what specific behaviors merit reinforcement.

- Remember that verbal praise is the most effective reinforcer. Use it often!

PART 2

PLANNING TO TEACH SPECIFIC DIRECTIONS

Have you ever asked a classroom full of students to begin a new activity only to end up with a stampede on your hands?

The answer is probably "yes." After all, during the course of a school day many situations arise that require students to "shift gears" and move in, out of, and about the room. These transitions can be a source of a lot of discipline problems. That's why you have to prepare for them before school begins.

Remember, the first rule of your Assertive Discipline Plan is "Follow directions the first time they are given." Therefore, you have to be sure that students understand the directions you ask them to follow. In the scene on the previous page, the students probably had every intention of lining up for recess—eventually. Unfortunately, no one told them *how* they were to line up.

In order to prepare students for changes in activities, you must teach them the directions that you want them to follow.

For example, here are directions you might teach students for lining up for recess:

1 When the recess bell rings, put away all of your papers, books and pencils.

2 When I call your row, stand up and push in your chairs.

3 Quietly walk to the door and line up. No talking.

It's up to you to make up your own list of classroom situations for which you need to determine specific directions. Your directions must reflect safety and logic, but they should also reflect your personal teaching style. The more clearly you understand the way in which you want your students to behave at each moment of the school day, the better managed your classroom will be.

Now consider some of the classroom activities for which you should teach directions. Read the list below. Check off any activities that apply to your own classroom. In the space given, add additional situations of your own.

☐ When the teacher is lecturing to the class

☐ When students are working in small groups

☐ When students arrive in the morning

☐ When students enter the classroom after recess

☐ When students need to go to the bathroom

☐ When students want a drink of water

☐ When students move from one activity to another

☐ When it is time for recess

☐ When the class goes to the school library

☐ When the fire drill bell rings

☐ When the class goes to a school assembly

☐ When students are on the playground

☐ When students are in the cafeteria

☐ When it is time to clean up

☐ When the class is having a discussion

☐ When students leave at the end of the day

☐ _____

☐ _____

☐ _____

☐ _____

☐ _____

☐ _____

☐ _____

Great start! You've identified the activities for which you need to teach specific directions. The next step is to write down the directions you want your students to follow. Read the simple guidelines and the examples given below.

Guidelines for Writing Directions:

• Choose three specific directions for each classroom activity.

• Your directions must be observable and easy for students to follow.

• Whenever possible, relate the directions to:

- The **materials** students should use.
- Whether students should be **in-seats** or **out-of-seats**.
- The **noise level** expected during the situation.

Examples of Specific Directions

Activity: When the teacher is lecturing to the class.

1 Clear desks of all materials.
   (materials)

2 Stay in your seat. Eyes on teacher.
   (in-seat, out-of-seat)

3 Raise your hand to ask or answer a question.
   (noise level)

Activity: When students are working in small groups.

1 Bring books, workbooks and pencils to groups.
   (materials)

2 When you get to your seat, begin the assignment.
   (in-seat, out-of-seat)

3 Raise your hand to ask or answer a question.
   (noise level)

Practice writing directions of your own for the activities listed below.

Activity: When students arrive in the classroom in the morning.

1 _____

2 _____

3 _____

Activity: When students enter the classroom after recess.

1 _____

2 _____

3 _____

Activity: When it is time for recess.

1 _____

2 _____

3 _____

Activity: When it is time to clean up.

1 _____

2 _____

3 _____

Activity: When the class goes to the school library.

1 _____

2 _____

3 _____

Now write directions for any other classroom activities you checked off or listed on page 23.

Activity: _____

1 _____

2 _____

3 _____

Activity: _____

1 _____

2 _____

3 _____

Activity: _____

1 _____

2 _____

3 _____

Activity: _____

1 _____

2 _____

3 _____

Activity: _____

1 _____

2 _____

3 _____

Activity: _____

1 _____

2 _____

3 _____

Activity: _____

1 _____

2 _____

3 _____

Activity: _____

1 _____

2 _____

3 _____

Activity: _____

1 _____

2 _____

3 _____

Activity: _____

1 _____

2 _____

3 _____

You've written your directions for different classroom activities. Now you must give some thought to how you will teach these directions to your students once school begins.

Plan Lessons for Teaching Directions

To successfully teach specific directions, you must plan a lesson just as you would for teaching a subject. If you've never done this before, it may seem time-consuming to plan a lesson for each direction you want to teach. But keep in mind that you are setting the stage for a smoother-running class. Put the time in now—and save time and energy all year long.

The sample lesson plan on the next page will give you some ideas for teaching directions to your students.

After reading the sample lesson plan, use copies of the open-ended worksheet on page 111 of the Appendix to help you plan the lessons you will teach your own students. Write a lesson for each activity for which you wrote directions. You will teach these lessons prior to the first time the activity takes place.

LESSON PLAN FOR TEACHING SPECIFIC DIRECTIONS

Objective: To teach students specific directions for _____

When to present this lesson: Teach directions for this activity prior to the first time the activity takes place.

Materials: _____
_____
_____
_____

These are the specific directions I will teach students for this activity:

1 _____
2 _____
3 _____

Procedure:
1 Write the directions on the chalk board. Have volunteer students read the directions aloud.

2 Explain your rationale. Tell students why it is important for them to follow these directions. Write your reasons below:
_____
_____
_____

3 Question students for understanding.

4 If appropriate, have students copy these directions in a designated section of their notebooks.

5 Have the entire class roleplay following these directions.
Alternate activity: Have one student play the role of the teacher and give the direction to the students.

6 Following the lesson, immediately begin the activity.

7 Review these directions prior to this activity taking place again.

LESSON PLAN FOR TEACHING SPECIFIC DIRECTIONS *See pages 28-29 for suggestions for use.* **111**

Sample Lesson Plan for Teaching Specific Directions

Objective: To teach students specific directions for a lecture activity.

**When to present
this lesson:**   Teach directions for this activity prior to the first time the activity takes place.

Materials: Notebooks, pencils or pens

These are the specific directions I will teach students for this activity:

1 Clean desks of all materials.

2 Stay in your seat. Eyes on teacher.

3 Raise your hand to ask or answer a question

Procedure: **1**   Write the directions on the chalkboard. Have volunteer students read the directions aloud.

2   Explain your rationale. Tell students why it is important for them to follow these directions.

"Let me tell you why these three directions are important. The first direction, "Clean desks of all materials is important because I will be handing out materials and you need to make room for them on your desks. The second direction, "Stay in your seat. Eyes on teacher" is important because it shows that you are paying attention to what I am saying. "Raise your hand to ask or answer a question" is important because if several students are talking at once, you and the rest of the class will not be able to hear me.

3   Question students for understanding.

4   If appropriate, have students copy these directions in a designated section of their notebooks

5   Have the entire class role-play following these directions.

Alternate activity: Have one student play the role of the teacher and give the direction to the students.

6   Following the lesson, *immediately* begin the activity to which the directions apply.

7   Review these directions prior to this activity taking place again.

ASSERTIVE DISCIPLINE IN ACTION
Teaching Specific Directions

- Teach directions for each classroom situation immediately prior to the first time the activity takes place. State the directions clearly to the students.

- Keep the lesson short—a maximum of 5-10 minutes.

- Question the students to make sure they understand your directions.

- Teach and use "start cues" such as: "When I say 'go,' I want you to put your books away," or "On the count of three, I want you to put your books away."

- Teach "activity names." This is important with younger students. Do they know what seatwork is? Do they know what ready groups are?

- Review the directions with students prior to each situation for the first few weeks of school. Thereafter, review the directions as needed.

- Whenever situations change, teach new directions.

- Review directions upon returning from long holidays.

- Reinforce students who follow directions by giving plenty of verbal praise: "Sara, your desk is cleared and you're ready to take your test. Good job following directions!"

CLASSROOM ORGANIZATION

Is interior design one of your job responsibilities? Yes! After all, the way in which you arrange your classroom and organize your materials has a direct impact on student behavior and learning. An effective classroom organization plan can go a long way toward preventing discipline problems.

- Are desks arranged so that you can easily work with individual students? Can you make eye contact with each student?

- Are materials organized so that you and students can get to them with minimal disruptions?

- Is your desk well stocked with the wide variety of supplies that are needed daily?

- Do you have an organized system for storing materials?

By carefully planning your classroom environment you can avoid some of the distractions that keep you—and your students—from functioning as effectively as possible.

Remember, your classroom is like a second home to both you and your students, so why not design the interior to be as comfortable, pleasant, workable and organized as possible? So get out your grid paper, pencils, scissors, files and boxes and let's get started tackling those classroom design dilemmas!

ARRANGING STUDENTS' DESKS

Desks and/or tables take up most of the space in your classroom. And students spend most of their time sitting in them, walking around them and working at them. That's why it's so important to think carefully about how you want to arrange your desks. There are lots of ways to do it. The arrangement you choose should fit the needs of your students and your own teaching style.

Guidelines for Arranging Desks

- Make sure all students can see the chalkboard (and you) from their desks. Good eye contact is important for both instruction and maintenance of behavior in the classroom.

- Allow aisle space for you to work with individual students at their desks. Long, connected rows of desks mean you could be disturbing one student while assisting another.

- If you teach to small groups (reading or math), provide for this as part of your room arrangement.

- Windows and doors can provide distractions for some students. If possible, avoid having desks face windows.

- Bookcases make great room dividers. Make sure they don't impair a student's view of you or the chalkboard.

- Place centers and work-area tables around the perimeter of the room.

- If talking is a problem, avoid having student desks face one another.

- Have one or two empty desks ready for new students. The first few weeks of school usually see the arrival of new students.

Look at the desk arrangements pictured below. Some will fit your teaching style and the needs of your students better than others.

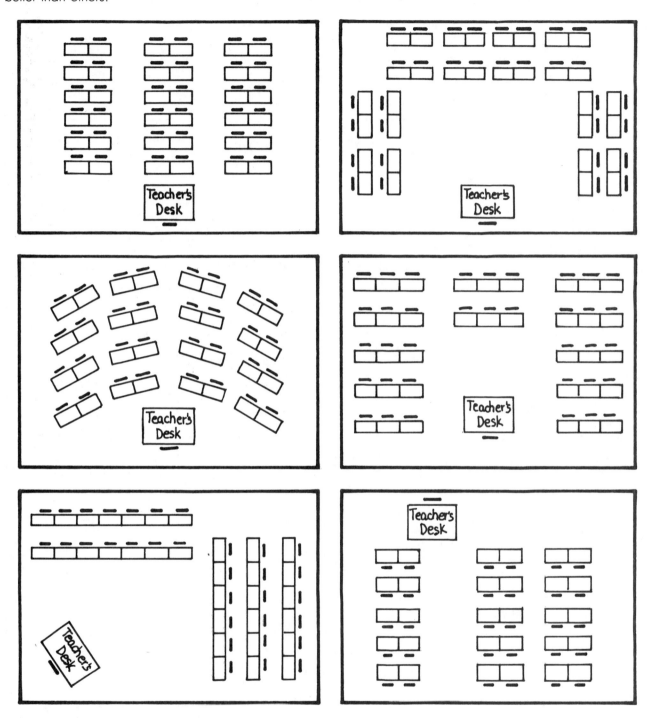

Plan before you move! Know ahead of time—before you go to your classroom—how you will arrange the desks. This will save you a lot of last-minute pushing, shoving and dragging of furniture! Use the grid paper (Appendix page 112) to lay out the arrangement of your classroom.

THE TEACHER'S DESK

Have you ever spent precious teaching time searching your desk for a "hidden" hole-punch or "missing" masking tape? It's not surprising! Your desk is the repository for everything under the sun—from rubber bands to extra buttons. To minimize class-time disruptions that can lead to loss of student attention and further discipline problems, you need to know exactly what supplies are in your desk and where each item is kept. Use the Teacher's Desk Checklist below to help you stock necessary supplies.

Teacher's Desk Checklist

☐ gradebook, lesson plan book
☐ seating chart
☐ substitute folder
☐ pencils, pens, markers
☐ erasers
☐ scissors
☐ hole punch
☐ ruler
☐ compass (for making circles)
☐ stapler and staples
☐ tape dispenser and extra roll of tape
☐ masking tape
☐ paper clips (both small and large)
☐ rubber bands
☐ pins (straight and safety), push pins, tacks, map pins
☐ glue, paste, rubber cement
☐ box of tissues
☐ bell
☐ whistle
☐ reward and incentive stickers
☐ rubber stamps and ink pads

☐ ready-to-use positive notes (Appendix pages 102-103)
☐ parent-teacher communication letters (Appendix page 151)
☐ birthday and get well cards
☐ notepaper
☐ teacher editions of textbooks
☐ oral reading book
☐ dictionary, thesaurus, almanac
☐ file folders
☐ clipboard
☐ clothespins
☐ loose coins
☐ teaching credential in a frame
☐ timer
☐ stopwatch
☐ knife, fork and spoon
☐ index file and cards
☐ sewing kit
☐ small tools (X-ACTO knife, staple remover, screwdriver, hammer)

DESKTOP ORGANIZATION

Not everything will fit inside your desk drawers. And there are some things that you will want to keep on top of your desk. Here are some ways to organize the teaching materials you want to keep at your fingertips:

Organize your papers. Stackable bins, corrugated cardboard shoeboxes, and wire dish racks or record racks can help you organize paper goods—from awards to parent letters.

Have often-used supplies close at hand. Cups, cans, boxes and baskets are excellent ways to organize your "stationery" materials such as pencils, pens, scissors, stamps, tape, and stapler. Decorate the containers with wallpaper leftovers, fabric, or colorful adhesive paper. Don't forget to label each container with its contents.

Put together portable supply boxes. Tackle boxes, plastic household carryalls, and plastic make-up cases (with sectioned areas) make perfect portable supply boxes. Include such items as pins, tape, glue, rulers, compass, hole punch, masking tape, paper clips, rubber bands, clothespins, and pointed scissors in your supply box. The portable supply box can be used at the teacher's desk or taken to another part of the room. For students who do not have these supplies at home, the portable supply box can be checked out overnight for special homework projects.

Carry your desk with you! Primary-grade teachers might also consider making a "supply apron." When you wear a supply apron, all the materials needed for both instruction and behavior plan implementation are right at your fingertips. Sew a row of pockets onto an apron and fill them with grading pencils, scissors, award stickers, marbles, erasers, etc.

STORING SCHOOL STUFF

"A place for everything and everything in its place." In the elementary classroom, these are really words to live by! Take some time before school begins to collect a variety of paper, plastic and metal containers. Choose containers for pencils, crayons, glue, markers and anything else you think you'll need to store, and label them. (Use the storage labels on page 113 of the Appendix.) When school begins, take your students on a tour of the classroom. Show them where school items are kept and explain that all items must be returned to these containers. Make sure that students understand all rules for using these items.

Pencil Problems?

Pencils can be a big problem in the classroom. "I can't find my pencil." "My pencil needs to be sharpened." "My eraser is gone." Solve this problem —and annoying interruptions—by implementing the "double duty" pencil policy. Get two cups (mugs, orange juice cans) and label them "sharp" and "dull." At the beginning of the day, the "sharp" container should be filled with sharpened pencils. As students need their pencils sharpened, they place their dull pencils in the "dull" container and take a sharp pencil from the "sharp" container. At the end of the day the pencil monitor sharpens all the pencils in the "dull" container and places them in the "sharp" container—ready for the following day.

* Keep your eyes open for a bargain on an electric pencil sharpener. It's fast and fun to use.

Crayon Crazy?

Crayons, like pencils, get dull too. Buy an eyebrow-pencil sharpener at the drug store. This makes a perfect crayon sharpener. Got a problem with lost crayons? Place last year's crayons and this year's crayon pieces in a basket. When students need a particular color, they borrow from the basket. Ask students to donate any broken crayons from home to the crayon basket.

Perplexing Paints?

Paints can be a messy problem. Collect margarine tubs with lids. Pour "student portions" of paint into the clean tubs and let your little Van Goghs go!

• Hint: Paint the tip of each brush with a different color paint. Students must use the correct brush with the correct tub of paint. This will cut down on the number of brown masterpieces.

• Hint: Styrofoam egg cartons make great paint palettes.

Searching for Scissors?

Ever go on the "great scissors search"? Buy a three-inch thick piece of styrofoam from an art supply store. Stick the scissors, blade side down, into the styrofoam and label it. This works for paintbrushes, too.

Clear Classroom Clutter!

Short on shelf space? Closet organizers are handy classroom organizers. Try these ideas:

• Hanging sweater bags are perfect for organizing and storing reams of writing, drawing, or art paper.

• Don't forget hanging shoe bags. Fill the pockets with glue, paste, tape, a stapler, hole punch, markers and a variety of other items. Label the pockets.

• Transparent shoeboxes and sweater boxes make it easy to view whatever is inside—from pipecleaners to pompoms.

• Invest in colored plastic hangers for students to hang their coats and sweaters on. Buy two colors—one for boys and one for girls. Or buy several colors to match group or cubby colors.

BIG Files for BIG Projects

Make poster-board folders to use for storing bulletin boards and art project samples. Place two sheets of poster board together. Tape three sides together with wide package-tape. Leave a long side open for easy insertion and removal of materials. Label the outside with a list of the contents. Make a poster board folder for every month of the school year. At the end of the month, or as you finish with them, place large materials into the folder.

Corrugated cardboard boxes can be used when filing three-dimensional items that won't fit into poster-board folders. If one box is too large for a single month's materials, use only four for the entire year. Label them Fall, Winter, Spring, and Summer and fill with materials from those seasons. Smaller boxes are also handy for storing unit materials.

Time Now to Save!

Don't be caught short of storage supplies when school begins. Start gathering those coveted containers now.

- juice containers
- variety of plastic, metal and paper containers
- 3" thick pieces of styrofoam
- hanging sweater bags
- hanging shoe bags
- styrofoam egg cartons
- margarine tubs
- colored plastic hangers
- sheets of poster board
- cardboard boxes
- other

_____

_____

_____

_____

_____

SETTING UP CENTERS

Do you have learning centers in your classroom? If you don't, you might consider setting up several this year. The most universal "center" in the elementary school classroom is the library or reading center. But don't stop there! Students can experience a variety of learning activities at these centers: writing, art, listening, subject-area and games.

Some teachers schedule center time into the daily program so that every student completes the center activity for the week. Other teachers use centers to provide follow-up on class-related activities for students who complete their work early. Whatever your reason, centers should be both challenging and fun. Make sure all the materials needed to complete the center activity are placed at the center. Then spend several minutes at the beginning of the day, or week, explaining each center's activity, showing the materials at each center, reminding where completed activities should be placed and reviewing how to behave at centers. It is very important that you spend time teaching the specific directions you expect students to follow at the centers otherwise discipline problems may arise.

When placed on the perimeter of the classroom, centers are not a distraction to students working at their desks or with the teacher. A table or desk might be placed at a designated center so students can complete the activity away from their own desks. Bookshelves make excellent center dividers and provide a place to display a sample of the activity to be completed. Clearly label each center. Use the rebus/word center signs provided on pages 114-117 in the Appendix.

ASSERTIVE DISCIPLINE IN ACTION
More Classroom Organization Ideas

Here are some additional classroom organization tips that will help you manage your students' behavior.

Discipline Clipboard to Go!

Students need to know they are responsible for their behavior outside of the classroom as well as in it. When you go with your class to the library, p.e., or assemblies, plan to take along a clipboard for recording names of students who are disruptive, and for documenting good behavior. When you return to your class, follow up with consequences and positives.

Time Out

There are times when you will find it necessary to have a student take "time out" in the classroom. Turn an extra desk toward the wall, or add a screen made from a packing box to the desk to make a private area for doing work or sitting quietly. The time-out area is advantageous because the student is not removed from the classroom and therefore does not miss out on important lessons.

PART 4

BACK-TO-SCHOOL BULLETIN BOARDS

Do you make the most of your classroom bulletin board and wall space? Bulletin boards can do a lot more for you than brighten up your room or serve as a backdrop for displaying student work. Bulletin boards can help you manage classroom behavior, organize your day's activities and encourage students to do their best work.

Use bulletin boards to your advantage. In this section of *Back to School with Assertive Discipline* we will be looking at four categories of bulletin boards. These include:

Positive Behavior Bulletin Boards

Bulletin boards that help keep individual students—and the whole class—on the good behavior track. Easy to make and fun to use.

Control Central Bulletin Board

Your classroom "command post." Control Central contains all the vital information you and your students need as you work through each day.

"Good Work" Bulletin Board

Start off the year by letting students know right away how proud you are of the good work they do. By highlighting student work, you reinforce positive work habits and provide examples of successfully completed assignments.

A-*door*-ables (Door Decorations)

Add a positive tone to your classroom environment before students go inside! Our A-*door*-ables let you get your message across right at the front door.

POSITIVE-BEHAVIOR BULLETIN BOARDS

On the first day of school you will display your Rules, Consequences and Rewards posters and introduce your students to your Assertive Discipline Plan. That's a great beginning! But there's more you can do to help insure that students comply with your behavior standards right away. Be prepared to "catch them being good" with an attractive and motivating positive behavior bulletin board.

Positive-behavior bulletin boards can be used to reinforce individual students or the whole class. Try these ideas:

Positive Bulletin Board For Individual Students

Brushing Up on Good Behavior

How to Construct:

• Use the "palette" master (Appendix page 118) to reproduce one palette per student. Have students cut out and write their names on the palettes. Palettes are then attached to the bulletin board as shown.

• The reproducible paintbrush (Appendix page 119) can be enlarged on an opaque projector. To use an overhead projector, trace the paintbrush onto a plastic sheet and then enlarge. (Many copiers have plastic sheets that can be used with the copier.) Trace the artwork onto sturdy white paper, color and then cut out. You may wish to laminate the figure or cover it with plastic vinyl sheeting. This will add durability and strength to the bulletin board piece.

Suggestions for Use:

Each time a student exhibits a predetermined "good behavior" (such as entering the classroom quietly after recess) allow him or her to color in one section of the paint palette. When all of the sections have been colored in, the student receives a reward.

Positive Bulletin Board
For the Entire Class

We Deliver Good Behavior!

How to Construct:

- Use the "piece of pizza" master on page 120 of the Appendix to reproduce 6 slices of pizza. Attach pizza slices to the bulletin board as shown.

- Draw a circle 15 inches in diameter on the board. This will be your pizza pan. Outline the pan with a thick-tipped felt marker. Use one of the pizza slices to trace pizza sections onto the circle.

- The reproducible "pizza delivery kid" (Appendix page 121) can be enlarged on an opaque projector. To use an overhead projector, trace the figure onto a plastic sheet and then enlarge. (Many copiers have plastic sheets that can be used with the copier.) Trace the figure onto sturdy white paper, color and then cut out. You may wish to laminate the artwork or cover it with plastic vinyl sheeting. This will add durability and strength to the bulletin board piece.

Suggestions for Use:

Each time the entire class exhibits a predetermined "good behavior" (such as lining up appropriately before school) add another slice of pizza to the pie. When the whole pizza is filled up, the class earns a special reward.

Option: Put up more than one pizza on the board so you can track different positive behaviors. Label each and add slices as students earn them.

For example:
   Pepperoni Perfect PE Behavior
   Good Listening Habits Pizza
   Extra-Special Lunchroom Behavior Pizza

You will find more bulletin board ideas like these in Lee Canter's *Bulletin Boards for Positive Behavior, Primary* and *Intermediate.*

"CONTROL CENTRAL" BULLETIN BOARD

"Control Central" will be the heart of your morning routine. Located close to the teacher's desk, this multi-faceted bulletin board combines the calendar, daily schedule, classroom helpers chart, homework habits charts, Assertive Discipline Plan (rules, consequences, rewards), daily homework assignments, class and school notices, birthday chart, weather station, and any other permanent activity you might wish to incorporate into the daily routine.

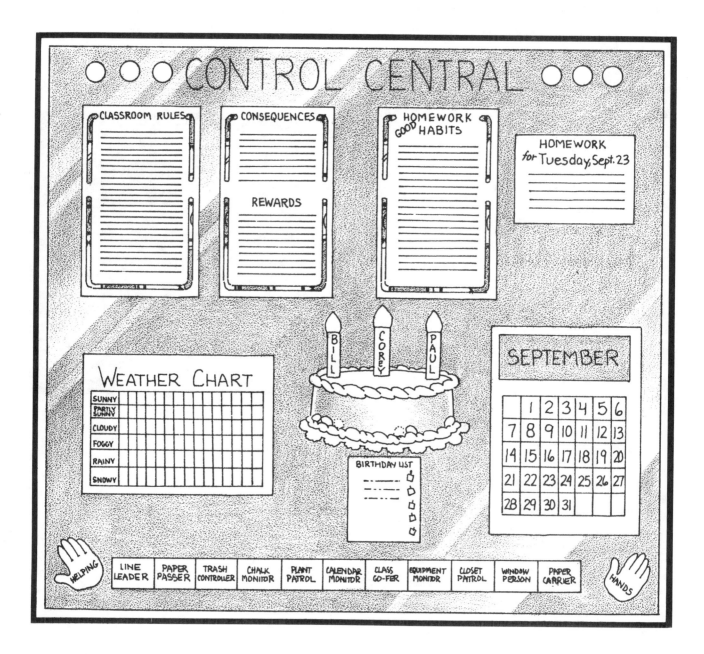

How to Set Up and Use Control Central

Control Central consists of a variety of classroom management components. Reproducible masters for many of these components can be found on pages 122-133 of the Appendix. Copy those pieces that you wish to use in your classroom and arrange them on a bulletin board (see suggested arrangement on page 44). Be sure to place them on a board that every student can see from his or her desk.

Each day, after welcoming the students and giving the flag salute, use "Control Central" as an interactive part of your morning routine.

Here are several suggestions that will help organize the classroom and set the tone for the rest of the day:

Creative Calendar Activities

Activities involving the calendar are an integral part of every primary classroom, but can be effective in upper grades, too. Purchase or make an open-ended calendar. Reproduce and cut out the appropriate Monthly Headliner (Appendix pages 125-128). Place at the top of the calendar. Then reproduce, cut and use the Date Markers(Appendix pages 122-124) to introduce everything from number recognition to math-facts practice. Write the numerals for each day of the month on the Date Markers. Then try some of these ideas:

• Place all Date Markers on the board, in order, numeral side down. Have a student name the day and date and then turn over the marker to reveal the correct numeral.

• Write a word, sentence or math problem on the blank side of each Date Marker. A student is selected to read the piece or answer the problem. If correct, that student has the privilege of turning over the marker.

Birthday Chart

A birthday is a very important day in the life of a child and should receive special recognition in class. Sometime during the first day of school, complete the Classroom Birthday List (Appendix page 129). Staple it to the inside cover of your lesson plan book. Place the birthday cake poster (Appendix page 130) on the board. Reproduce the birthday candles (Appendix page 131). Write the name of each September birthday student on a candle, with the date of the birthday in the candle flame. Cut out and pin all of the September birthday candles to the cake. Whenever a student's birthday arrives be sure to give special recognition with a card and classroom chorus of "Happy Birthday".

Handy Helpers Chart

Library pockets are excellent for use on the Helpers Chart. Write the job titles (or place the cards on page 132) on the front of each library pocket. Write each student's name on an index card. At the beginning of the week, assign classroom jobs by inserting name cards into pockets. At the end of the week, write the helper job on the back of the student card. This helps to keep tabs on job distribution.

Weather Station

It is the weather person's responsibility to note the weather outside and report it to the class. Duplicate one weather chart (Appendix page 133) per month. Place the chart on the "Control Central" board. After the weather person has reported the weather, he or she colors in the appropriate square on the weather chart. At the end of the month determine how many days were sunny, cloudy, rainy, etc.

Additional "Control Central" Components you may wish to add to your bulletin board:

Classroom Discipline Plan Posters
        (Appendix pages 98-101)
Good Homework Habits Chart
        (Appendix pages 158-159)
Daily Homework Assignment Sheet
        (Appendix page 160)
Daily Schedule
        (Appendix page 171)

"GOOD WORK" BULLETIN BOARD

When you use a bulletin board to display classroom assignments or homework that is done well, you provide positive reinforcement and demonstrate to students what constitutes an appropriately done assignment. All students enjoy having their good work posted for others to see.

Designate one bulletin board to showcase outstanding examples of student work. Plan to display student work as soon as possible at the start of the year. Remember to write a positive comment on each displayed paper.

Try this "blue ribbon" bulletin board idea:

Reproduce copies of the blue ribbons on Appendix page 134. (Use bright blue paper, of course!) Staple a blue ribbon to the corner of each paper you display. As the year goes on, keep a record of "Blue Ribbon" papers. When a student has received five (or any designated number) of ribbons, present that student with a "Blue Ribbon Certificate" (Appendix page 135). Be sure to change papers frequently, displaying everyone's work over a period of a few weeks.

Here are some bulletin board headline ideas you can use. Change throughout the year to highlight different categories of work.

- Blue Ribbon Work

- Prize-Winning Papers

- Homework Hall of Fame

- Blue Ribbon Book Reports

- This is a First-Class Class!

- All-Star Homework!

A-DOOR-ABLES
Back-to-School Door Decorations

On the first day of school the first impression your students (and parents) have of you begins at the classroom door. So why not start out on the right foot and decorate the door in a festive, fun, imaginative way? Information on the door should include the teacher's name, grade, room number, first and last name of each student in the class, and an inviting theme and phrase. Choose a theme appropriate for the grade level and let your imagination run wild. Here are a few "a-door-able" suggestions:

School is a "Lotto" Fun!

Place a lotto card (Appendix page 136) on the door of your classroom. Upon arrival, each student writes his or her name in one of the lotto boxes. When all the students have arrived, remove the lotto card from the door. Then throughout the day pick winning lotto numbers from a box. Winners receive "school supply" prizes such as pencils, erasers, pads of paper, etc.

Come On In and Park It!

Reproduce the cars (Appendix page 137) on colored paper. (A variety of colors will look great.) Write the name of a student on the license plate of each car and arrange on the classroom door.
Suggested headlines:
Come On In and Park It! at (Ms. Smith's) Garage
You "Auto" Know You're in the Right Place!

Mr. Sign Man

Mr. Sign Man (Appendix pages 138-139) can hang around your door all year long. He's very versatile. He'll hold up class lists, clever slogans and a cache of other framables. Have fun with this classroom character; dress him up for the holidays: a mask at Halloween, a pilgrim hat at Thanksgiving, a stocking cap in winter. Use this friendly mascot to help you get your messages across!

ASSERTIVE DISCIPLINE IN ACTION
Time-Saving Bulletin Board Ideas

Bulletin boards should be a year-round part of your behavior management and teaching routine. These time-saving ideas can make it easy!

Easy Seasonal Changes

Cover your bulletin boards with three layers of paper—orange, red and yellow. The orange background will work with your fall bulletin boards: September, October, and November. The red background fits into the holiday and winter themes of December, January and February. And sunny yellow is the perfect background for your spring bulletin boards from March through June.

Year-Round Good Behavior

Year-round bulletin boards save time and energy. For example, make a "Good Behavior Tree" in September. Draw a tree with several branches radiating from the trunk. Then fill the branches from month to month with a variety of good behavior items—apples for September, yellow, orange and red leaves for October, pumpkins for November, ornaments for November, snowflakes for December and so on. Children who earn a predetermined number of good behavior points, get their names written on the apples, leaves, etc.

Involve Students

Select one bulletin board to be totally student created. Time lines, book report projects, arts and crafts activities, literature-based ideas—all designed, created and displayed by students. Form monthly bulletin-board committees whose responsibility it is to plan and execute a "bulletin board of the month." And don't forget to take pictures of the end results. A photo display of these bulletin boards at spring Open House builds super self-esteem.

GETTING PARENTS ON YOUR SIDE

One of the most important goals you can set for yourself this year is to get more support and backing from parents. Research has clearly shown that when parents are involved, a child does better academically and behaviorally. You owe it to students and to yourself to get parents on your side. You need their support. You deserve their support. Take steps now to make sure you get their support!

In Part 1 you were given guidelines for sending home your Assertive Discipline Plan. That's a great start. But there's more you can do right now to ensure that parents will be there when you need them.

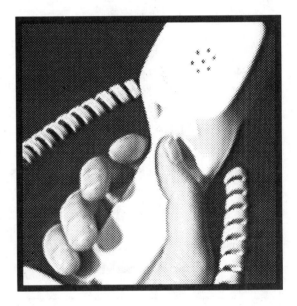

It's up to you, as a professional educator, to reach out to parents and encourage their participation. Keep in mind that parents may not even recognize the important role they play in their children's education—or what they can do to help.

In this section of *Back to School with Assertive Discipline* we will examine some strategies you can implement before school begins and at the start of the school year.

SEND OUT THE WELCOME WAGON!

The sooner you make contact with your new students and their parents, the better. By communicating with students and parents *before* school begins you are making them aware of your commitment to the upcoming school year.

Introduce Yourself!

Sometime during the summer, write a note (Appendix page 140) or postcard to each student, introducing yourself and expressing your excitement about the upcoming school year. Tell the student how much you are looking forward to meeting him or her. You may want to include a snapshot of yourself, perhaps from vacation. This will make you seem a lot more familiar and a lot less threatening on the first day of school.

Send the welcome wagon out to parents, too. Write an informal note (Appendix page 141) briefly stating your pleasure at their child being in your class and how you are looking forward to a successful year together. You might also take this opportunity to tell parents something about yourself and your general expectations for the upcoming year.

Host a Before-School-Begins Get-Together

You may even wish to host a before-school get-together. Invite both parents and students. Explain the first week's routine, give a tour of the classroom, and use the opportunity to get to know each other. The atmosphere should be relaxed and friendly. Serve cookies and punch and enjoy!

Pick Up the Phone!

If writing notes or hosting get-togethers are not your style, "reach out and touch" your new students and parents by phone. Introduce yourself, remind students of the day and exact time school begins, ask about their vacation—in short, get acquainted!

CREATE A BACK-TO-SCHOOL PARENT HANDBOOK

A parent handbook is a great way to give parents a lot of school-related information in one package. Teachers who have created the Handbook report that it's a well-used resource—and much appreciated by parents. Collect information that you think would be of interest to parents. (Many teachers include such varied items as magazine articles on child development, nutrition tips, and district curriculum guidelines.) The Handbook should reflect you, and the messages you want to get across to parents.

Here is a list of items you might want to include in your handbook.

Parent Handbook Checklist

- ☐ class list
- ☐ staff list, school address, phone number, school hours
- ☐ map of the school
- ☐ a note about yourself
- ☐ your Assertive Discipline Plan
- ☐ your homework policy
- ☐ daily classroom schedule
- ☐ grade level curriculum
- ☐ manuscript or cursive writing guide
- ☐ school/calendar year showing all school holidays and non-teaching days

- ☐ blank teacher/parent communication forms (Appendix page 151)
- ☐ policies about absences, medical appointments, making up class work
- ☐ "How to Help Your Child Study at Home" tip list (Appendix page 147)
- ☐ suggested reading lists
- ☐ health concerns (nutrition, exercise, sleep)
- ☐ volunteer letter (Appendix page 148)

Once you have gathered all your material for the Handbook, reproduce the pages on colored paper. Add a cover sheet (Appendix page 142), staple the pages together, and distribute during the first week or two of the new school year.

Parent Handbook Updates

Ever run across articles, cartoons, or important information you'd like to pass along to parents? Plan to keep a "Homework Handbook" file all year long. Add material as you come across it and then incorporate into next year's handbook.

MAKE "BACK-TO-SCHOOL" NIGHT A PARENT INVOLVEMENT SUCCESS

Back-to-School Night can be the most important night of the school year. It's your opportunity to meet parents, explain your policies and programs in detail, answer any questions about your class, and assure parents of your commitment to their children. This is the time to make allies of parents. Make the most of it!

Guidelines for encouraging parents to attend:

• Send out Back-to-School Night invitations (Appendix page 143).

• Hold a Back-to-School Night raffle. Parents who attend get to place raffle tickets in a jar (Appendix page 144). During the next school day, the teacher pulls out several winning raffle tickets. School supplies (markers, pocket dictionary, compass) make excellent prizes. Be sure to tell students about the raffle so they can help motivate their parents to participate.

• Hold Back-to-School Night Lotto. Have parents sign in on a lotto card (Appendix page 145). Each parent who attends Back-to-School night writes his or her name in a space on the lotto board. (If two parents attend, they should both sign the same space.) The teacher pulls winning numbers the next day and awards prizes to students whose parent's names were drawn.

• Motivate students to motivate parents to attend by involving students in preparing some of the Back-to-School Night activities (see suggestions on the next page). This can help generate enthusiasm that they can pass on to parents.

And once they're there . . .

1. Make sure you write an outline of the topics you will be talking to parents about. This is no time to get nervous and leave out important information! Be sure to include an explanation of your Assertive Discipline Plan and homework policy. It is vital that parents understand their role in both these areas. Above all, remember this: Parents' number-one concern is that you are concerned about their child. Listen carefully to their questions. If necessary, take notes and follow up with a phone call or written message.

2. Give a slide presentation (or video) showing students in their daily classroom routines—entering the classroom, working in small groups, doing independent seatwork, moving to centers, cleaning up after an art activity, exercising during P.E., reviewing homework assignments, or demonstrating positive behaviors. Don't forget to include a group shot of the entire class. Make sure every student appears in the slide show.

3. Play a tape recording of students discussing classroom activities. Once again, include everyone in the tape.

4. Have each child leave a note written to his or her parent. The note is left in the child's desk. At Back-to-School Night the parents read the notes and write a return message to be found by their child the next morning.

5. Have students tape record a song to be played for parents. Then at Back-to-School Night have parents sing and record a song to be played for students the next day.

6. Hand out a packet of information that parents can take home with them. If Back-to-School Night is scheduled shortly after school begins, it's a good time to distribute copies of your Parent Handbook.

7. Spend several minutes at Back-to-School Night explaining how volunteers will be used in your classroom. Encourage parents who have special interests they'd like to share with students to contact you. (See page 58.)

Back-to-School Night Follow Up

Let parents know how much you appreciated their participation in Back-to-School Night. In a few days, send a brief "Looking Back at Back-to-School Night" note home (Appendix page 146). Use the opportunity to thank parents for coming and to update them on any item that might have come under discussion at Back-to-School Night. Because it's sometimes difficult for parents to speak up and air their concerns in front of a whole group, the parent note also includes a section where parents can respond to you with any questions they may have. This follow-up is also an excellent way to make contact with parents who did not attend Back-to-School Night.

INVITE PARENTS TO TAKE AN ACTIVE PART IN THEIR CHILD'S EDUCATION

Recent research shows that the more interest parents display in their children's education and the more actively they support the school's efforts, the better chance those students have to achieve academic success. It is part of your professional responsibility, then, to encourage parents to be involved.

Helping at Home

Many parents want to help their child do better in school, but they just don't know what to do. You can help by giving parents a list of specific ways they can help their children learn at home. Write a list of suggestions on the open-ended "How to Help Your Child at Home" sheet (Appendix page 147). The checklist on the following page will get you started on ideas. You'll be able to think of many more that will meet the particular needs of your students. As students progress though the year, send home new information that pertains to current classwork. Parents and students will soon recognize the sheet as as a helpful home teaching aid.

"Helping Your Child at Home" Checklist

- Read aloud to your child. Research has proved that this is *the* most important thing a parent can do to ensure a child's reading success.
- Have your child read to you.
- Do shared reading. You read a sentence. Your child reads a sentence.
- While in the car have your child read street signs and billboards.
- At the market have your child read product labels.
- Obtain a library card for your child and check out a book.
- Encourage your child to read the newspaper. Discuss articles together.
- Measure objects and rooms in the house together.
- Subscribe to child-oriented magazines. Read them together.
- View television programs together. Discuss them afterwards.
- Create flash cards for your child's particular needs—alphabet recognition, vocabulary words, numbers, math facts, states and capitals, etc. Use flash cards in a variety of game activities.
- Have your child follow a recipe, measure ingredients and prepare a dish.
- Begin a story and have your child finish it.
- Using magazines, go on a phonics picture-hunt looking for pictures of things that begin with specific letters.
- Go on a color, shape, or number walk. Your child points out things that are a particular color or shape, or counts items such as trees, houses and mailboxes.
- Have your child figure change from the grocery or department store.
- Encourage your child to write stories on a typewriter or computer.
- Play games on the refrigerator with magnetic letters and numbers.
- Writes notes to your child. Place them around the house—on the bed, on the door, on the mirror, in a lunchbox.
- Have your child write letters and thank-you notes to friends and relatives.

Helping at School

Volunteers can be a great help to you in your classroom. Think about the kind of help you'd like to receive from parents (start jotting down your list in the spaces below). Then send home a volunteer request letter (Appendix page 148) the first week of school. Make sure you offer some creative alternatives for working parents who can't be in the classroom during the school day (they like to help, too!) Ideas might include creating posters for the classroom or helping out on a Saturday "classroom improvement" project. And don't forget to ask parents what *they'd* like to do. You just might have a talented storyteller, musician or puppeteer among your parents.

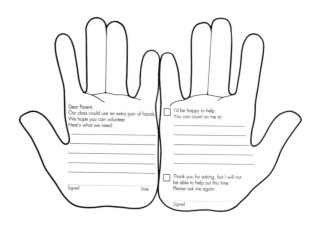

I could use parent help in these areas:

_____

_____

_____

_____

_____

_____

_____

Planning for Your Volunteers

When school begins, make your volunteers welcome by designating a table, or special location, as the volunteer area. Show them where coats and other personal belongings can be stored during class time. Introduce the volunteer to the class, explaining to the students what help he or she will be giving.

Your volunteers are a valuable asset. As their "manager" it is up to you to see that their time is used to best advantage. Your volunteers will be asked to do a variety of jobs—from clerical help (stapling, recording grades, filing student work) to instructional and activity assistance (tutoring, supervising art projects, chaperoning field trips, helping students with written work). Plan their time wisely. Explain the job clearly, make your expectations known, and then write the specific task in a spiral notebook. Don't forget to place basic items such as pencils, erasers, pens, scissors, a spiral notebook, and an oversized apron at the area. A volunteer should not have to go hunting, or disturb you, looking for necessary items.

A Note of Thanks

As the school year goes on, let your volunteers know how much their assistance is appreciated by both yourself and the students. Recognize the volunteers' good deeds with thank-you notes (Appendix page 149) and special cards. Send volunteers cards during the holidays, signed by all your students. Sometime towards the end of the school year, plan to invite all your volunteers to a special "Thank You" luncheon, prepared and served by the students (put it on your long-range planner now!).

SEND HOME A WEEKLY CLASSROOM NEWSLETTER

Inform parents about classroom activities and upcoming events. But don't do all of the work yourself! This method of communication will be even more effective if students help create it. Here are two ideas:

Primary grades: Weekly Family Letter

Every Friday each student writes three or more sentences telling what they did during that week. The sentences are turned in and the teacher compiles them into one big letter (typed) making sure that a sentence from each child is included. The letter is addressed to "Dear Family." On Monday, the teacher gives each student a copy. Students underline the sentence they wrote and take the letter home to show to parents.

Send a note home to parents with the first Weekly Family Letter. Make sure they understand that this letter will be a weekly group effort, and that their child's writing will be included each week. Suggest that they ask their child to read the whole letter to them each week and spend some time talking about the events recorded in the letter.

Keep all of the weekly letters in a three-ring binder. As the weeks go by, students will enjoy looking back at their classroom experiences. You may wish to occasionally add photographs to liven up this very lively history.

Upper grades: Family Newsletter

Older students will enjoy having a hand in planning and producing a weekly (or bi-weekly) newsletter. As a group, decide on regular columns that will be included. Assign a committee to be responsible for gathering the information for and writing each column. Rotate assignments throughout the year.

Suggestions for columns:

> A Message from the Teacher
> We're Proud of These Students!
> Upcoming Projects and Assignments
> Special Events

SPREAD THE GOOD NEWS!

Too often, parents hear from teachers only when there's a problem. Let's reverse that trend! Reinforce positive student behaviors through frequent notes, happygrams, awards and phone calls to the home. Every student should take home at least one positive acknowledgement a week—for good homework habits, excellent classroom behavior, or special recognition of any kind. (See the reproducibles on pages 102, 103 and 155 of the Appendix.) Keep a record of positive phone calls and notes home so you can make sure all students receive equal attention!

MAKE YOURSELF ACCESSIBLE TO PARENTS

Set aside one morning and one afternoon a week to talk with parents, either in person or on the phone, who have concerns about their children. Come to school fifteen minutes earlier than usual and stay a half hour later. Encourage parents to visit or telephone you on those days. As a reminder of the school's phone number and your special "conference" days, reproduce and give each parent one of your own teacher calling cards. Just fill in your name, room number, school name and phone number on the Teacher Calling Cards on page 150 of the Appendix. Hand these out at Back-to-School Night or send home at the beginning of the school year.

DOCUMENT ALL PROBLEMS

Plan ahead for dealing with behavior problems: In order to present an accurate, professional picture of students' behavior, you must keep accurate records of how students behave in your class. When dealing with parents regarding any kind of problem, you must be able to base your statements on factual data. The more documentation you have, the easier it will be to get parents to listen. Try this idea: Keep a file box on your desk filled with index cards—one for each student. Jot down the following information whenever a behavior problem occurs: 1) date, 2) time, 3) place, 4) rule broken, 5) action taken.

ASSERTIVE DISCIPLINE IN ACTION
Phoning Parents with Good News!

What a surprise it is for parents to answer the phone and hear positive news from their child's teacher! Get into the habit of phoning parents with good news and it won't be so difficult to call them when there is a problem to be solved. You'll have already established a comfortable relationship, and parents will be much more likely to listen to what you have to say. The first week of school isn't too soon to begin using this very effective parent involvement technique.

Sample Positive Phone Conversation

Teacher: Hello, Mrs. Paul? This is Miss Jones, Amanda's teacher.

Mrs. Paul: What did she do wrong?

Teacher: She didn't do anything wrong. As a matter of fact, I'm calling to tell you that she's done very well this first week of school. She did all of her classwork and handed in her homework assignments.

Mrs. Paul: I can't believe you're calling me to tell me she's doing well. I'm so used to hearing about nothing but problems about Amanda.

Teacher: Well, I believe it's just as important to tell parents when their child is doing well in school as it is when they're doing poorly.

Mrs. Paul: I wish all teachers were like you.

Teacher: I'd just like to add that I really am pleased to have Amanda in my class this year. And I'm looking forward to working with you to make sure that she gets the most out of this school year. I'm so glad we've had this chance to get acquainted over the phone!

PART
6
PLANNING FOR HOMEWORK

Was homework a headache for you last year? Too many incomplete assignments? Not enough cooperation from parents? You're not alone. Recent Gallup Poll statistics show that the most frequently recurring problem in school is homework. And problems with homework can lead to other discipline problems. When a student feels poorly about his or her performance in one area, the result can be a lack of self-esteem that shows up in other areas. Unfortunately, homework is too often just such a catalyst. But it doesn't have to be that way. Properly handled, homework can be an arena for success—a chance for students to reinforce skills learned in class, develop responsibility, and work to their full potential. It all depends on how you approach it—from the very beginning of the school year.

So take a deep breath and relax. Homework doesn't have to be a hassle if you "set the stage" properly.

Teachers who have an effective approach to homework lay the foundation for student success by first developing a homework policy. A homework policy clearly states your expectations for everyone involved in the homework process: student, teacher *and* parents. Use time *before* the school year starts to formulate and write out your homework policy. Include it with your Parent Handbook or send it home in letter form during the first two weeks of school. Students should receive a copy soon after school begins— before they are assigned their first homework.

Note: Homework guidelines should not be part of your classroom rules. They are not part of your Assertive Discipline Plan.

DEVELOPING YOUR HOMEWORK POLICY

Your homework policy should address each of the seven points listed below. Think carefully about each one. Remember, this policy will guide the way you, your students and their parents handle homework all year long.

A homework policy should:

1. Explain why homework is assigned.

   You can't assume that parents or students understand why homework is given or how important it is. You need to explain the benefits of homework and why you are going to assign it. For example:

   • It reinforces skills learned in class.

   • It prepares students for upcoming class topics.

   • It teaches students to work independently.

2. Explain the types of homework you will assign.

3 Inform parents of the amount and frequency of homework.

4. Provide guidelines for when and how students are to complete homework.

5. Let parents know how you will positively reinforce students who complete homework.

6. Explain what you will do when students do not complete homework.

7. Clarify what is expected of the parent.

Take a moment to go over the sample parent letter on the next page that explains a typical fifth-grade homework policy. Then use the Homework Policy Planner on page 66 to write down information that will help you organize your own homework policy.

Sample Homework Letter to Parents

To the family of _____ ,

I believe homework is important because it is a valuable aid in helping students make the most of their experience in school. I give homework because it is useful in reinforcing what has been learned in class, prepares students for upcoming lessons, extends and generalizes concepts, teaches responsibility and helps students develop positive study habits.

I will assign homework Monday through Thursday nights. Homework should take students no more than one hour to complete each night, not including studying for tests and long-range projects. Spelling tests will be given each Friday. I will give students at least one week's notice to study for all tests, and one written report will be assigned each grading period.

I expect students to do their best job on their homework. I expect homework to be neat, not sloppy. I expect students to do the work on their own and ask for help only after they have given it their best effort.

I will check all homework. I strongly believe in the value positive support plays in motivating children to develop good study habits. I will give students praise and other incentives when they do their homework.

If students choose not to do their homework, I will ask that parents begin checking and signing completed homework each night. If students still choose not to complete their homework, they also choose to lose certain privileges. If students choose to make up homework the next day, their homework will be accepted but they will receive a one-grade reduction on that assignment. If they choose not to make up missed assignments, students will receive a fifteen-minute detention for each homework assignment missed. The first time a student receives a detention for missed homework, I will contact the parents.

If there is a legitimate reason why a student is not able to finish homework, the parent must send a note to me on the day the homework is due stating the reason it was not completed. The note must be signed by the parent.

I feel that parents are the key to making homework a positive experience for their children. Therefore, I ask that parents make homework a top priority, provide necessary supplies and a quiet homework environment, set a daily homework time, provide praise and support, not let children avoid homework, and contact me if they notice a problem.

Please read and discuss this homework policy with your child. Then sign and return the bottom portion of this letter to school.

We can do this—together!

Your signature

Homework Policy Planner

Why do you assign homework?

_____

_____

_____

What are the types of homework you will assign?

_____

_____

How often will homework be assigned?

_____

_____

What guidelines will you give students for completing homework?

_____

_____

_____

How will you positively reinforce students who complete homework?

_____

_____

_____

What consequences will you impose when students do not complete homework?

_____

_____

_____

What are the responsibilities of parents in the homework process?

_____

_____

_____

How will homework affect a student's grade?

_____

_____

Now use the information on this sheet to write your homework policy letter to parents.

BACK UP YOUR HOMEWORK POLICY

Just as you must back up your Assertive Discipline Plan by teaching specific directions, you must also be prepared to back up your homework policy by teaching students *how* to do homework effectively. You have to give students the skills and tools they need if they are to fulfill their homework obligations appropriately.

Teach Homework Skills

Many teachers assume that students come to class knowing how to get homework done. Don't assume anything. Students need to be taught homework skills, just as they need to be taught math facts and spelling words. These skills should be taught during the first two weeks of school before any academic homework is assigned. The time spent in teaching these skills will pay off throughout the school year.

Lessons that should be taught include:

• Introducing the homework policy
Students must learn exactly what is expected of them regarding homework.

• Setting up a study area at home
Students must understand that to do homework successfully they must have a place in which to work.

• Creating a Homework Survival Kit
To complete homework assignments effectively, students must have available at home a collection of basic materials.

• Returning homework to school on time
Remembering to bring homework assignments back to school when they are due is an important responsibility students must develop.

On the next pages you will find lesson suggestions for teaching these skills. Prepare yourself now by making copies of the reproducible activities listed and plan how and when you will present the lessons.

Introducing the Homework Policy

Tell students that you are going to give each of them a written homework policy to take home. Explain that a homework policy is a list of standards that will help students *and* parents understand their homework responsibilities. Read the policy standards to the class. Explain why a homework policy is needed (so parents and students alike will clearly understand your expectations about homework). Tell students about the positives you will use when homework is done appropriately. Explain the consequences that will be imposed when homework is not done. Check for student understanding by having them paraphrase each of the standards you read. Finally, give each child a copy of the homework policy to take home to parents.

Assignment: Explain to students that they are to read the homework policy with their parents that night. Tell them that after reading the policy together, you want the students and their parents to sign it and return the signature portion to school. Explain that their signatures will let you know that parents and students understand what is expected of everyone regarding homework.

Setting Up a Home Study Area

Students will do a better job on homework if they have an appropriate place in which to study, and if they have all necessary supplies at hand. Encourage students to study in a quiet, well-lighted place, as free from distractions as possible. Explain to students that this place can be anywhere—the kitchen table, the library, or at after-school care. It doesn't matter where the location is as long as it's quiet and conducive to studying. Ask students to share ideas about where they can do their homework.

Classroom Activity: Have each student decorate a Study Space Poster (Appendix page 152). Completed posters are used to designate the place the student has chosen as the study area at home.

Putting Together a Homework Survival Kit

Students often have trouble doing assignments at home because they don't have the necessary supplies on hand. The Homework Survival Kit Checklist (Appendix page 153) is a useful guide to the types of supplies that are most often needed to complete homework assignments. Run off copies of the Checklist and send home to parents. Explain to students that just as they need materials in class to get their work done, they also need materials at home to do homework.

Classroom Activity: Ask students to each bring a shoebox (or similarly sized box) to class. Have students decorate the boxes and label them "My Homework Survival Kit." Tell students that they are to take these kits home to keep homework supplies in. Review the Homework Survival Kit Checklist. To get things started on the right foot, give each child a pencil and eraser to "inaugurate" the kit.

Returning Homework on Time

Nothing is as frustrating to young students as getting a homework assignment done—and then leaving it at home. It happens all the time. Help students develop responsible homework habits by giving them a little organizational nudge. Talk about the importance of leaving completed assignments in the same place each night. Share ideas about where this might be (in a backpack, by the front door, on the kitchen table). Tell students that if they always leave their work in the same place, pretty soon they'll get into the habit of always picking it up there on the way out the door in the morning.

Classroom Activity: Ask each student to choose a "Homework Drop Spot" at home where they will leave completed assignments. Reproduce copies of the Homework Drop Spot sign (Appendix page 154). Have students color the signs and take them home to designate their very own Homework Drop Spot.

REINFORCE GOOD HOMEWORK HABITS

It is very important to reinforce good homework habits with praise and other positive motivators. The motivators on pages 155-157 of the Appendix will show your students that you've noticed their good habits.

A Season of Good Cheer Bookmarks

When these monthly characters peek from between the pages of a book, they remind the student of a job well done. Run 30 copies of each (page 155) and you've got a 4-month supply of homework motivators.

You've Got Good Homework Skills All Locked Up

Students who use the keys to good homework habits (returning homework on time, doing homework all by yourself) are given this award (Appendix page 156) and a chance to unlock the Good Homework Habits treasure chest. Fill a large, lidded box with items from the Homework Survival Kit. Put a chain around the box and secure with a lock and key. Place the key and two others on a ring. The student gets one chance to unlock the treasure chest by choosing the correct key and opening the lock.

Desktop Award Charts

Let your students chart their homework progress on the Dinosaur desk chart Appendix page 156). For each day a student returns an acceptable homework assignment, the student colors in (or adds a sticker or stamp to) a box on the chart. When all the boxes are filled, it can be taken home as a reward for good homework habits. Another "special treat" can be presented along with the award chart—a small toy, a special activity coupon, or a favorite snack.

Be a Coupon Clipper

Reward good homework habits by attaching a Class-Act Coupon (Appendix page 157) to a student's completed homework assignment. These special treats are great incentives to "keep up the good work."

POST YOUR HOMEWORK STANDARDS!

For students to meet your expectations about homework, you must define how you expect students to complete their assignments. The Good Homework Habits poster (Appendix pages 158-159) will remind your students—every day—what your standards are regarding homework. Write your homework rules on the poster and hang it in the classroom where it can be easily seen by students. Typical expectations:

- All assignments will be completed.

- I will do homework on my own.

- I will turn in work that is neatly done.

- I will turn in homework on time.

- I will make up homework missed.

POST WRITTEN INSTRUCTIONS FOR ALL HOMEWORK ASSIGNMENTS

How many times have you heard this excuse: "I didn't do my homework because I couldn't remember the assignment." Verbal homework instructions are <u>not</u> sufficient for all of your students. Solve this problem by designating a bulletin board (or part of Control Central) as your Homework Tonight spot. Use the Homework Chart (Appendix page 160) to post daily or weekly homework assignments. At the end of the week, place the week's homework charts in a binder. This becomes a handy reference for students who were absent.

Students can also record all homework assignments on the convenient Homework Sheet (Appendix page 161) Use a felt-pen to fill in the subject areas at the top of the chart. Write the spelling list for the week in the right-hand column. Reproduce and hand out Monday morning. Students record homework assignments in the appropriate boxes. The Homework Sheet should be kept in a special homework folder or envelope that goes home every night. A parent signature line is included at the bottom of the page.

ASSERTIVE DISCIPLINE IN ACTION
Contacting Parents About Homework Problems

Probably the most common mistake in working with parents is that teachers do not contact them about a problem until the problem is out of hand. As soon as you realize a student is having problems with homework that necessitates involving the parents, call them.

Before contacting parents, plan what you will say. Follow these guidelines:

- **Describe the behavior that necessitated your call.**

Describe in specific, observable terms what the child did or did not do:

"I am calling because I'm very concerned about Kristin. She did not turn in three homework assignments this week."

- **Clearly spell out what you have already done to help the child.**

- **Describe what you want the parent to do.**

Always preface what you want the parent to do with the statement, "It is in your child's best interest that we work together to help him (her).

- **Indicate your confidence in your ability to solve the problem if the parent works with you.**

Let the parent know that his or her support is critical.

"I am sure that if we work together we will be able to motivate your child to do homework on his own."

- **Tell the parent that there will be follow-up contact from you.**

Let the parent know that you will not let the issue drop, and that you will be in touch within one week to inform the parent if the situation has or has not improved.

PART
7

FINAL PREPARATIONS

Preparations are winding down. The room is invitingly arranged to greet students and their parents on opening day. Supplies have been gathered and organized. Creative bulletin boards flank student desks. You've outlined your Assertive Discipline Plan and prepared a homework policy that will encourage good homework habits and independent study. You're all ready? Well, not quite.

It's time to take care of those "last-minute" specifics that will make the beginning of the school year really special. Careful planning is the order of the day for the first days of school! Remember, you want to project an attitude to students that says, "I'm in charge." That means you must be organized and know exactly what you're doing—down to the minute. The first days of school can be tough for students and teacher alike. You will find that many discipline problems can be avoided altogether if you are well-prepared and focused.

SELECT FIRST-DAY ACTIVITIES

The first day of school should be fun for students and teacher! Choose activities that will interest students and also get everyone started on a productive school year. Here are some ideas:

Ice Breakers

Students love to get back to school to see their old friends and to make new ones. Don't assume that all students know each other. Plan to play name games, do name puzzles, and make name visors to promote "getting acquainted."

Getting to Know You

Have all students write 3-5 things they would like their fellow students to know about them. This could be information, thoughts, feelings about themselves, their family, their experiences, their future plans, etc. (I was born in Salt Lake City. My mother and I planted a vegetable garden this summer. My favorite place is the observatory. I want to be an astronomer and study the stars. I get my hair color from my grandpa whose nickname was "Red.") Collect the lists and place them in a box. Read each paper, one clue at a time. See if other students can guess who the clues are about.

Memory Names Game

This is a progressive memory game. Have students form a circle. One student begins by saying, "Mrs. Jones's (teacher's name) students are named (student says his or her name)." The next student repeats the phrase, but adds his or her name to the list. For example, "Mrs. Jones's students are named Laura and Bill." When someone misses a name on the list, the students in the circle introduce themselves, one at a time. "Hi, my name is Laura. Hi, my name is Bill." The game starts all over again with the person who missed.

Name Visors

Have students make and decorate visors (Appendix page 162) with their own name on the front. After cutting out and putting together the visors, collect them. Then redistribute visors, but not to their original owners. Students put visors on without looking at the name. The object is for each student to find out whose visor he or she is wearing by listening to clues given by other students. Some clues might include:

"You were in Mr. Ross's class last year."

"You are wearing a yellow shirt today."

"You desk is in the front of the room."

Searching for Names

Make up a wordsearch or crossword puzzle using the names of the students. Have students circle the names of people they already know with yellow crayon, and those students they don't know with green. As follow-up, each student must poll all "green" students about their favorite food, animal, sport and television show.

Beat the Clock

Have students sit in a circle. Set the timer or watch the clock for a minute (or any predetermined time). Have each student name the students in the circle as quickly as possible. The object of the game is to name all of the students in the circle before time is up.

Writing Activity

Let's put a twist on the proverbial "first day" writing assignment. Instead of having students write about what they did this summer, allow their imaginations to take over. Reproduce page 163 of the Appendix and find out what students wished they had done this summer (gone to the moon, surfed in Hawaii, visited cousins on the farm). Also find out what students are glad they didn't do this summer (swim with piranhas in the Amazon, windsurf in the Arctic). Brainstorm with the class before you hand out the assignment.

Play "Back to School" Bingo

This bingo game is perfect for learning names, reviewing skills, or just plain having fun. It can be adapted to fit any grade level. Give each student a blank bingo card (Appendix page 164). Depending on the subject you choose for the game, each student writes 16 choices in the bingo squares. For example, 16 names of classmates, 16 states, 16 letters, or 16 addition facts. When all the bingo cards are completed, you pull names, states, letters or numbers from a box. Students mark squares with the correct answer. Played like regular bingo.

Plan an Art Activity

Don't attempt anything too involved on the first day of school. The only materials your students will need for the Magic Square activity (Appendix page 165) are a pair of scissors and some glue. Reproduce the page on white paper. Students cut out the shapes and form pictures by attaching to pieces of paper. Many designs are possible, but the house and dog configurations are shown at the bottom of this page. When students have devised their "magic" pictures, have them glue the pieces in place on a piece of colored construction paper.

Make Personal Calendars

The first day of school is a "red letter" day for most students. Keep track of this day—and the rest of the year—by having students make and use their very own calendars. Reproduce copies of the open-ended calendar on Appendix page 166. Have students write in the name of the month, fill in dates, then use the calendar for writing down upcomming school events, a favorite activity each day, or any other personal information they may want to fill in.

SELECT SPECIAL FIRST-WEEK ACTIVITIES

Accent the first week of school with special activities that will pique students' interest. Here are some ideas:

Create Time Capsules

A lot of personal growth takes place during one school year. Students change tremendously from September to June. Make that change apparent by letting students create their own individual "time capsules."

Have students bring in a container (coffee can, shoebox, sturdy envelope) during the first week of school. This will serve as the time capsule that will hold a variety of papers, pictures, and memorabilia from the start of school. Ask students to include some of the following:

- a headline from this week's newspaper

- an article from the newspaper

- a list of their favorites: TV show, movie, recording artist, song, book, subject, color, friend, food, soda pop, etc.

- a flower or leaf wrapped in plastic wrap

- an example of their handwriting

- a written paragraph describing the teacher and their fellow classmates

- a personal item from home

- a recent photograph

- a piece of string measuring the student's height

- a list of goals the student wishes to accomplish by next June

Each student places the items in the container. All containers are collected and placed in a class "time capsule" such as a garbage can, large box, or pillow case. This container is placed in storage until the last week of school when it is "unearthed." Students will be amazed at the many different ways they have changed during the school year.

An Autobiography—in Pictures!

This fill-in booklet allow students to write and draw about the subject they know most–themselves. The 8-page booklet (Appendix pages 167-169) can be completed as a class project, or at a center as an independent activity. Finished booklets make great additions to "get acquainted" bulletin boards—perfect for "Back-to-School" Night.

MAKE 3-D DESK TAGS

Stand-up desk tags are easy to read–from anywhere in the room. Duplicate the "back-to-school" crayon tags (Appendix page 170) on sturdy construction paper or index stock. Using a broad marker, write each student's name on both sides of the tag. Cut along dotted lines (on crayon heads), fold and staple. Place the name tags on individual desks. The first few minutes of the class will run much more smoothly if students are assigned seats before they enter the room.

PREPARE LESSON PLANS FOR THE ENTIRE FIRST WEEK

At no time during the year is this motto more true–"Be prepared!" So gather your resource books, teacher's editions, and your wits, and carefully prepare your lesson plans for the first week of school. Follow these procedures:

1. Make a list of everything you want to accomplish with your students the first week of school.

2. Transfer these activities to your lesson plan book. Overplan for each day. Introduce information, lessons and activities in their order of importance.

3. Once the *week* is planned, transfer your plans to the Daily Schedule (Appendix page 171). This schedule breaks the teaching day into 30-minute increments.

On the following pages are some suggestions for activities you might wish to include in your first week's lesson plans.

Suggested First-Day Activities

- Introductions – teacher, students, staff.
- Take attendance and lunch count.
- Explain morning routine pattern.
- Tour the classroom.
- Play name games.
- Play "get acquainted" activities.
- Tour of schoolgrounds (show restrooms, office, playground, cafeteria).
- Explain your Assertive Discipline Plan.
- Teach specific directions to different activities as those activities arise.
- Practice fire drill.
- Assign cubbies, lockers, etc.
- Distribute materials (pencil, crayons, rulers, etc.).
- Read aloud to students (material depends on grade level).
- Do simple exercises to music.
- Teach a subject-area lesson with a follow-up art activity.
- Assign students to guide new students around school.
- Have students complete a personal inventory.
- Play "20 questions."
- Sing songs.
- Play "Back-to-School" bingo.
- Do a creative writing activity.
- Complete a wordsearch or puzzle.
- Explain "Control Central."
- Do a "birthday" count for the birthday chart.
- Introduce children to your special "attention-getting" signal.
- Hand out parent handbooks, parent letters, notes from the office.

Suggested First-Week Activities

Continuation and review of activities, rules, and procedures from first day, plus:

- Continue introducing classroom procedures.
- Review classroom rules each day.
- Write a positive note to every child in class.
- Introduce classroom helper jobs. Assign positions.
- Have students complete "All About Me" book (Appendix pages 167-169).
- Review previously taught skills.
- Administer teacher-developed diagnostic tests.
- Give subject-area lessons that are geared towards all students.
- Have students choose free-reading books.
- Create your first Family Newsletter (page 60).
- Play reading and math games.
- Make time capsules (page 77).
- Begin teaching homework skills (pages 67-69).
- Continue to review specific directions for classroom activities.
- Begin sending home positive notes to parents (Appendix page 103).

REPRODUCE ALL WORK PAPERS FOR THE FIRST WEEK

It's time to make friends with the photocopier or duplicating machine! Run off at least five extra copies of each reproducible worksheet or activity you plan to use during the first week. Clip all copies of the same master together. Then, referring to your lesson plans, place paper "piles" in the order you will using them.

In the space below, make a list of all the reproducibles you need to copy for the first week of school.

_____

_____

_____

_____

_____

_____

_____

_____

_____

_____

_____

_____

_____

_____

_____

_____

_____

_____

_____

_____

_____

Are You Ready?

Use this handy checklist to determine if you're ready for the first day.

☐ Door poster in place with name tags or class list?
☐ Bulletin boards?
☐ Room and desks arranged?
☐ Teacher's desk stocked?
☐ Supply containers and cabinets filled and labeled?
☐ Pencils sharpened?
☐ Student supplies ready to distribute?
☐ Name tags on cubbies?
☐ Stamps, stickers, positive reinforcement rewards ready?
☐ Awards, coupons, notes reproduced and cut apart?
☐ Calendar pieces cut apart, numbered and placed on bulletin board?
☐ Parent Handbook or parent letter reproduced (collated)?
☐ Assertive Discipline Plan prepared?
☐ Homework Policy established?
☐ Parent-Involvement Plan created?
☐ Supply containers and cabinets filled and labeled?
☐ Lesson plans ready for the first week?
☐ All papers reproduced for the first day?
☐ Daily schedule written on board?
☐ Name tags on student desks?
☐ Documentation file prepared?

First Day of School Agenda

List everything you need to carry out the door with you the first day of school and jot down any last-minute reminders to yourself.

ASSERTIVE DISCIPLINE IN ACTION
Assertive Discipline Review

Before heading back to school, take a few minutes to review the basic Assertive Discipline concepts that will enable you to successfully manage behavior in your classroom.

Assume an Assertive Attitude

In order to manage student behavior effectively, your words and actions must reflect an assertive attitude:

"I am the boss in the classroom. I have a right to teach. My students have a right to learn. No student will stop me from teaching or another student from learning."

Know Your Assertive Discipline Plan

To maintain and support your assertive attitude you have planned ahead of time what you will do when students misbehave. This was accomplished by developing an Assertive Discipline Plan.

Teach the Assertive Discipline Plan

Before using the plan, teach it to your students. Carefully explain the rules, disciplinary consequences, and positive reinforcements so that students will know what is expected of them and what the consequences of their behavior will be.

Implement the Assertive Discipline Plan

Consistency is the key to the success of your Assertive Discipline Plan. As soon as students understand the plan, start using it daily.

PART
8

BACK TO SCHOOL!

It's all right to be a little anxious and nervous on the first day of school. But you have nothing to fear if you're organized, prepared and have a positive attitude. Arrive at school early. Double-check your lesson plans to make sure you have everything ready. Check with the office to see if any new students have been enrolled in your class. Prepare desk and name tags for those students. Take a deep breath and relax.

When you greet students at the door the first day, keep in mind that your classroom management begins at that moment. In order to manage student behavior effectively, your words and actions must reflect an assertive attitude. Ask yourself these questions:

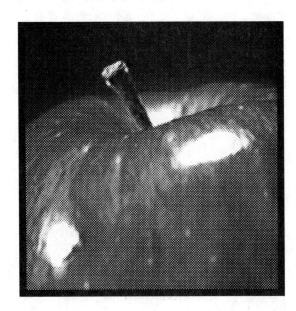

- Do I feel as if I am the boss in my classroom?

- Do I stay calm whenever students misbehave? (I do not yell or become hostile.)

- Do I tell students what I want just one time? (I do not repeat myself over and over again.)

- Do I know exactly how I will use my Assertive Discipline Plan to deal with students who choose not to follow the rules of the classroom?

Remember: You have the right to expect students to behave in your classroom. Your Assertive Discipline Plan will help you handle discipline problems calmly and effectively without getting upset or angry.

On the following pages are some suggestions that will ease you through the first days of school.

THE FIRST DAY

Many parents bring their children to school on the first day to make their children more comfortable and to meet the teacher. Take advantage of this situation. Introduce yourself to both student and parent and make them feel welcome. Announce to parents the time school will be dismissed or have the information posted.

A Picture Perfect Beginning

Are you a"shutter-bug?" If so, have your camera ready to snap photos of incoming students. When having the film developed, ask for double prints. These photos serve as "get acquainted" bulletin board pieces as well as behavior motivators. Pictures can be placed on cubbies, autobiographies, holiday greeting cards and inside the "first-week-of-school time capsule."

Before school begins, cut a large star from yellow poster board. Take a picture of each student holding the star. At the end of each day, choose two "star" behavior students. Place their photographs on the bulletin board.

Start the First Day Assertively

Communicate your expectations immediately. Let students know that you are in control from the very beginning. A solid foundation for the entire school year is built on the strength you project on the first day of school.

Introduce Your
Assertive Discipline Plan

The sooner students know your expectations for classroom behavior, the better. Before school began, you completed three posters—Classroom Rules, Consequences, and Rewards (Appendix pages 98-101). Refer to each chart as you teach the rules of expected behavior, explain what will happen when a student chooses not to follow the rules, and discuss the rewards a student can expect when rules are followed.   Refer also to the Implementation Guidelines on page 20.

This procedure works well when introducing your Assertive Discipline Plan:

1. Read the rule. (For example, "Raise your hand and wait to be called upon before you speak.")

2. Demonstrate the proper way to raise your hand.

3. Have a student role-play the proper way to raise his or her hand.

4. Have the entire class role-play the proper way.

5. Explain and demonstrate what will happen when a student chooses not to follow the rule the first time, second time, third time, fourth and fifth time.

6. Share several of the ways students will be positively rewarded for following the rules (individual, group and classwide incentives).

Follow Up with the
"Building Good Behavior" Booklet

As a follow-up to your Assertive Discipline Plan presentation, have students make their own "Building Better Behavior" booklets (Appendix page 172). Depending on the grade level, have students copy the rules, consequences and rewards in their mini-booklets from your classroom charts. For younger students, write the information in the booklet before you duplicate the page. Students then take the booklets home and discuss the information with their parents. Booklets are signed and returned to class where they are kept on file or inside the students' desk.

Use Positive Reinforcement Frequently

Let your students know from the first day that you will support their appropriate behavior with verbal praise, awards, and special activities (refer to pages 13-16 for specifics). When giving verbal praise, make it as specific as possible and directed toward the behavior you are trying to cultivate in the classroom. For example, "Thank you for raising your hand and waiting to be called upon before speaking, Jennifer."

Begin Teaching Specific Directions

In Part 2 of this book you learned how important it is to teach students the directions you want them to follow for various classroom activities. You wrote directions and planned lessons. This is the time to begin teaching those lessons! Remember, you must teach each lesson prior to the first time the activity takes place. For example, teach students how to line up for lunch before they line up the first day. Review and reinforce daily thereafter until you are sure all students know what is expected of them. Remember to give students plenty of positive reinforcement for following directions correctly.

Send Students Home with a "Special Delivery" Envelope

Starting with the first day of school and continuing throughout the year, students will be taking home notes, newsletters, flyers, menus, awards, homework, corrected assignments and a variety of other papers. Here's a way to ensure that those papers get home and messages from parents get back to you.

Purchase a 9" x 12" manila envelope for each student in your class. Write the students' first and last names on the envelope. Staple a blank calendar on the front. Place all papers to go home in the envelope. Have the parent initial the date on the calendar, place all returning paperwork in the envelope and send it to school with the child. Send the "special delivery" envelope home every night. Even if you have nothing to send home, parents might have absence notes, lunch money, or parent-teacher telegrams (Appendix page 151) to send to you. And remember to send home at least one positive note a week per student.

At the end of the first day, ask yourself these questions:

1. Were any students absent today? If yes, be prepared for their arrival. For the first week, have a folder placed on each empty desk. When papers or supplies are handed out, put an extra set at each vacant desk. Returning students or new enrollees will then have a set of those all-important first week papers when they begin class.

2. Could I use an extra pair of hands this week? Enlist the help of a parent to help minimize classroom interruptions.

3. Were there any student seating arrangements that might cause potential behavior problems? Sometimes it's apparent from the outset that some students are catalysts for poor behavior. Move them immediately. Seat them closer to the front of the room—and you!

Things to do for tomorrow:

_____

_____

_____

_____

_____

_____

_____

_____

_____

_____

_____

THE FIRST WEEK

During the first week of school, you will be establishing the rules and routines that students will be following for the rest of the year. Spend an adequate amount of time teaching the rules and routines, role-playing these behaviors, and reviewing them. Use lots of positives whenever you see students choosing to follow the rules. And when new students enter your class, explain your discipline plan in detail. When these behaviors become second-nature to your students, a smoothly run classroom will be your reward.

Positive Picture-Taking

To illustrate classroom rules (especially for non-readers), take pictures of students performing appropriate behaviors. Mount the photos on the rules charts, next to the corresponding written rule.

Be a "P.R." Person

Practice "P.R." (positive reinforcement) every day. Here are several activities and awards that will start your students on the road to great behavior:

Good Behavior Bonuses

To positively reinforce individual students who follow classroom rules, hand out these "back-to-school" badges, bookmarks and acorns (Appendix page 105). Run off numerous copies at the beginning of the week and keep them nearby.

- Badges can be pinned to clothing or attached to a length of yarn or string.

- Big oaks from little acorns grow. Plant an acorn seed every time you see good behavior being practiced. Hand out acorns to individual students. When a student has received three (or any predetermined number of) acorns, a special reward, coupon or treat is given to the student.

Start the Year with SQIRT

In order for students to become better readers, they need time to read. Start the school year by implementing SQIRT time in your classroom. SQIRT stands for SUSTAINED QUIET INDEPENDENT READING TIME. During SQIRT time everyone should read—even the teacher. Make SQIRT a part of your daily routine. After lunch recess, students enter class and read silently for 15 minutes.

Rainbow Reader Club

Start a Rainbow Reader Club in conjunction with SQIRT time. Reproduce one Rainbow Reader sheet (Appendix page 173) for each student. When SQIRT time is over, each student fills in a square on the reading rainbow for each page read. Each row of squares is colored the same—the bottom row red, then orange and so on. When the entire rainbow is colored in, a reward is given.

Something Is Bugging Me!

To avert problems before they escalate, give students a way to let off steam. Have these notes (Appendix page 174) available so students can make an appointment with you to discuss a problem.

Teach Good Homework Habits

During the first week of school, begin teaching your students the good homework habits (refer to pages 67-69) they need to follow throughout the school year.

Designate a box, bin or file where completed homework is placed. Post your homework policy on a bulletin board (or at Control Central). Review your homework policy and reinforce good homework habits every day. Reward good homework habits with positives, but also remember to follow-through with consequences when students choose not to follow your homework policy.

At the end of the first week, ask yourself these questions:

1. Has every student received positive reinforcement during the week, both verbal and written? If not, determine why some students are choosing not to follow the rules or expected behaviors. Is it the seating arrangement? Are your rules too vague? Have you taught these skills? Have you consistently followed through on the consequences and rewards of your discipline program? By all means, contact the parents of a student who is causing problems. Don't wait until scheduled parent conferences. Enlist their help right from the beginning.

2. Have you prepared or adjusted your lessons so that every student in the class can feel successful? If lessons are too hard the first week of school, some students might get "turned off" for the rest of the year. Make these lessons motivating and creative without being too challenging. You have 39 more weeks to challenge them. Spend this week making students feel good about themselves. During the week, you should have evaluated each student's abilities. By next week, students can be placed in reading and math groups according to their abilities.

3. Have you started your SQIRT program? If you don't have reading books in your classroom, schedule a visit to the school library for the beginning of next week and start your independent reading program then.

4. Do you have students who need extra assistance? Ask your principal about cross-age tutors or the school volunteer program. Have your volunteer desk ready for your helpers.

THE SECOND WEEK AND BEYOND

After the first week of school, take time to evaluate the rules, routines, desk arrangements, procedures, and time schedules that are not working. Determine why they aren't effective and decide how to alter them to make them workable. Have a plan of action ready before you make changes. And don't change everything at once! Confusion is not the order of business during the first month of school. Make adjustments and changes gradually, but do make them.

These are not working:

_____
_____
_____
_____
_____
_____
_____

This is how I will change them:

_____
_____
_____
_____
_____
_____
_____

Make a Permanent Seating Chart

By now you have likely worked out any seating arrangement problems. Fill out a permanent seating chart in pencil and keep it in your lesson plan book. Students love to play "musical chairs" when you're absent. Nip this practice in the bud by making a copy of your seating chart and placing it in a substitute file along with the copy of your Assertive Discipline Plan.

Keep Your Positive Reinforcement System Fresh

The key to the success of your discipline program is the motivation of positive reinforcement. Keep your positive reinforcement system fresh by adding new awards, activities, and ideas all through the year. Change the motivational bulletin boards frequently. Display different good homework papers every day. Use stamps and stickers appropriate to the season and holiday. (See Lee Canter's *Fall, Winter, Spring* and *Summer Motivators.*) Change marbles in a jar (page 15) to pennies in a piggybank. Hand out "best-behavior baseballs" during the World Series and "super-behavior snowcones" at the onset of summer. Variety is the spice of this system, so keep your shelves well stocked!

ASSERTIVE DISCIPLINE IN ACTION

Consistency is the key to successful classroom behavior management. As the year progresses, you may find yourself asking some of the questions listed below. If so, feel free to take this book out again and go over Part 1.

- **Do I consistently praise and reward students who follow the rules of the classroom?**

- **Do I consistently impose consequences on those students who choose not to follow the rules?**

- **Do I consistently change my positive reinforcement system to keep it fresh and motivating?**

- **Do I consistently send home positive notes to the parents of all students?**

- **Do I consistently contact parents as soon as a problem arises?**

Together we've completed a step-by-step process for preparing for the new school year. Hopefully we have addressed the issues that have caused you problems in the past. Remember, be consistent, be confident and, above all, enjoy the year to come.

APPENDIX

Reproducibles for Part 5—Getting Parents on Your Side

Reproducibles for Part 6—Planning for Homework

Reproducibles for Part 7—Final Preparations

Reproducibles for Part 8—Back to School!

CLASSROOM RULES POSTER *See page 10 for suggestions for use.*

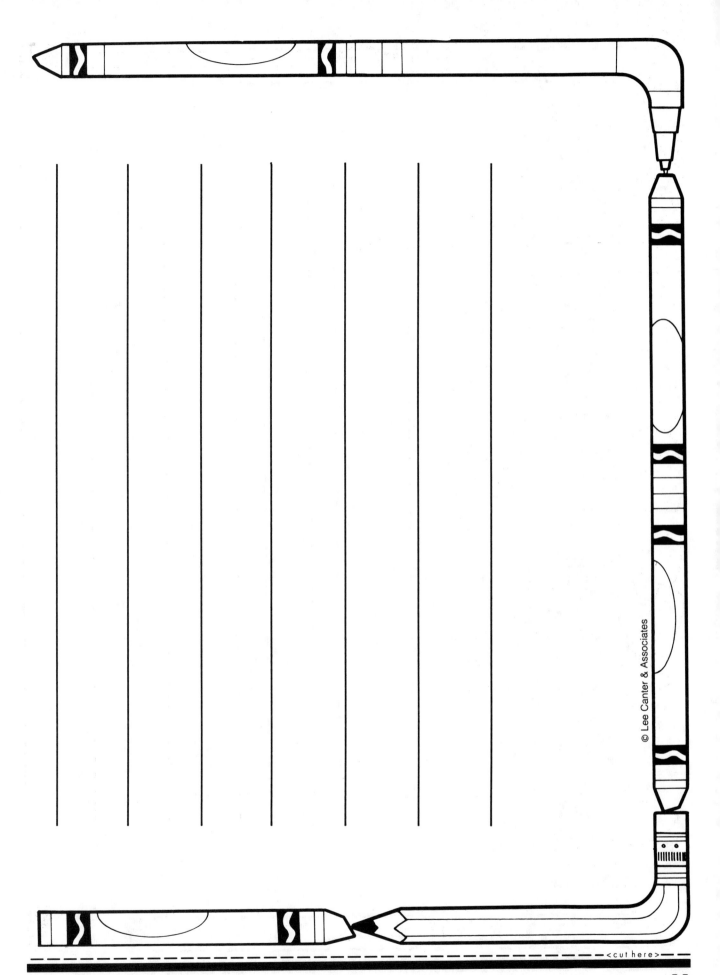

—< c u t h e r e >——

REWARDS POSTER *See pages 13-16 for suggestions for use.*

To _____

HERE'S THE SCOOP!

Your behavior is front-page news because _____

_____

_____

_____

Signed   Date

- - - <cut here> -

To _____

Your behavior has been a real treat!

Thanks

HOT DOG!

You're Great!

Signed   Date

- - <cut here> -

Dear_____,

Thought you'd like to know that

_____'s

behavior has been outstanding because

_____

_____

_____

Signed _____ Date _____

© Lee Canter & Associates

--- <cut here> ---

Dear_____,

_____

followed all the classroom rules today.

Signed _____ Date _____

© Lee Canter & Associates

--- <cut here> ---

School is COOL when you follow the RULES!

Student's name _____

 © Lee Canter & Associates

– – – < cut here > –

_____'s

Student's name

behavior has been "doggone" great!

Signed _____ Date _____

© Lee Canter & Associates

GOOD BEHAVIOR BONUSES

To positively reinforce students who follow classroom rules, hand out these awards frequently. Make an effort to recognize all of your students several times each week.

Name

I was caught

being good.

© Lee Canter's Assertive Discipline

super behavior in school!

Name

© Lee Canter's Assertive Discipline

You're Terrific!

Good Job!

Thanks!

- -<cut here>- - -

Classroom Messenger

YOU EARNED IT!

1st in Line

YOU EARNED IT!

Free Time

YOU EARNED IT!

Reading Time

YOU EARNED IT!

5 Minutes with Teacher

YOU EARNED IT!

YOU EARNED IT!

Teacher's Assistant

YOU EARNED IT!

YOU EARNED IT!

YOU EARNED IT! COUPONS   *See page 14 for suggestions for use.*

<fold here>

Best Behavior Desk

<cut here> <cut here>

<fold here> <fold here>

I've been on my best behavior!

© Lee Canter & Associates

<fold here>

Dear Parent,

I am delighted that _____ is in my class this year.
We can all look forward to many exciting and rewarding experiences as the year progresses.

As I firmly believe that life-long success depends on self-discipline, I have developed a Classroom Discipline Plan that gives every student the opportunity to manage his or her own behavior. Your child deserves the most positive educational climate possible for academic growth. Therefore, this plan will be in effect at all times.

Classroom Rules

1 _____

2 _____

3 _____

4 _____

5 _____

To encourage students to follow the classroom rules, I reinforce appropriate behavior with

_____

If a student chooses to break a rule, these are the consequences:

1st time _____

2nd time _____

3rd time _____

4th time _____

5th time _____

Severe Disruption _____

I have discussed the Classroom Discipline Plan with my students, but I would appreciate it if you would also review the plan with your child, then sign and return the form below. I will be communicating with you frequently throughout the year to keep you aware of your child's progress. Please feel free to contact me at any time.

_____   _____   _____
Teacher's Signature   Room Number   Date

— — <cut here> —

I have read your Classroom Discipline Plan and discussed it with my child.

_____   _____   _____
Parent/Guardian Signature   Child's Name   Date

— — <cut here> —

DISCIPLINE PLAN WORKSHEET

Teacher _____ Grade _____ Room _____

Rules—Behavior Rules for My Classroom

1 _____

2 _____

3 _____

4 _____

5 _____

Consequences—When a Student Breaks a Rule

1st time _____

2nd time _____

3rd time _____

4th time _____

5th time _____

Severe Clause _____

Rewards—Positives I Will Use When My Students Behave

_____

_____

_____

_____

_____

Principal's Comments _____

_____

_____

_____

SUBSTITUTE'S PLAN

From the desk of: _____

Dear Substitute:

The following are the guidelines for the Discipline Plan used in my classroom. Please follow them exactly, and leave me a list of students who break the rules and a list of students who behave properly. Thanks.

Classroom Rules

1 _____

2 _____

3 _____

4 _____

5 _____

Consequences

When a student breaks a rule:

1st time _____

2nd time _____

3rd time _____

4th time _____

5th time _____

Severe Clause: If a student exhibits severe misbehavior such as fighting, open defiance, or vulgar language, the following consequence is to be immediately imposed:

_____

Students who behave will be rewarded when I return with:

_____

_____

I appreciate your cooperation in following my Discipline Plan.

Sincerely,

LESSON PLAN FOR TEACHING SPECIFIC DIRECTIONS

Objective: To teach students specific directions for _____

When to present this lesson: Teach directions for this activity prior to the first time the activity takes place.

Materials: _____

_____

_____

These are the specific directions I will teach students for this activity:

1 _____

2 _____

3 _____

Procedure: **1** Write the directions on the chalk board. Have volunteer students read the directions aloud.

2 Explain your rationale. Tell students why it is important for them to follow these directions. Write your reasons below:

_____

_____

_____

_____

3 Question students for understanding.

4 If appropriate, have students copy these directions in a designated section of their notebooks.

5 Have the entire class roleplay following these directions.

Alternate activity: Have one student play the role of the teacher and give the direction to the students.

6 Following the lesson, *immediately* begin the activity.

7 Review these directions prior to this activity taking place again.

— —<cut here>— —

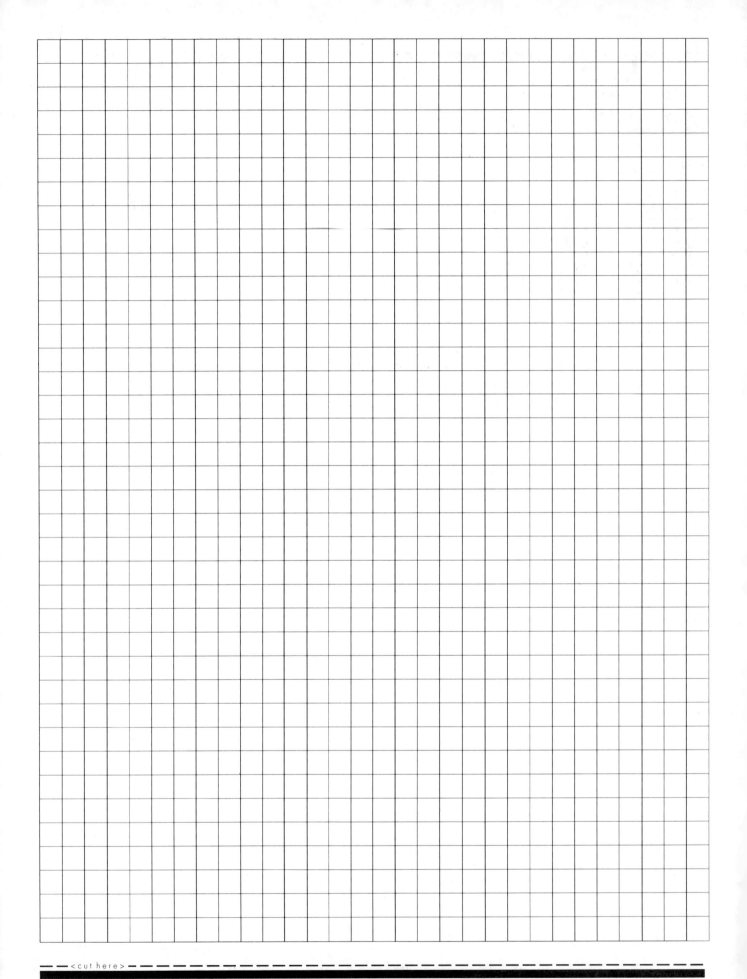

paper

pencils

crayons

markers

colored pencils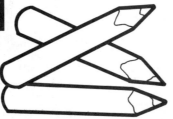

paints

water- colors

paint- brushes

glue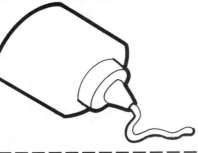

paste

lunches

scissors

Games

Listening

A R E A

A R E A

CENTER SIGNS *See page 39 for suggestions for use.*

Social Studies

Art

A R E A

A R E A

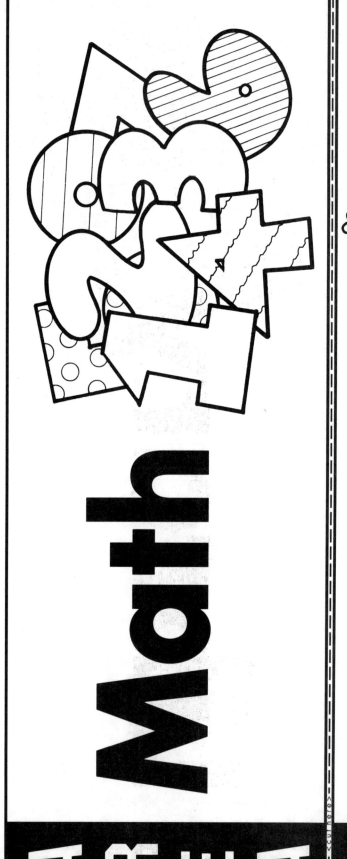

Math

A R E A

Science

A R E A

Writing

Library

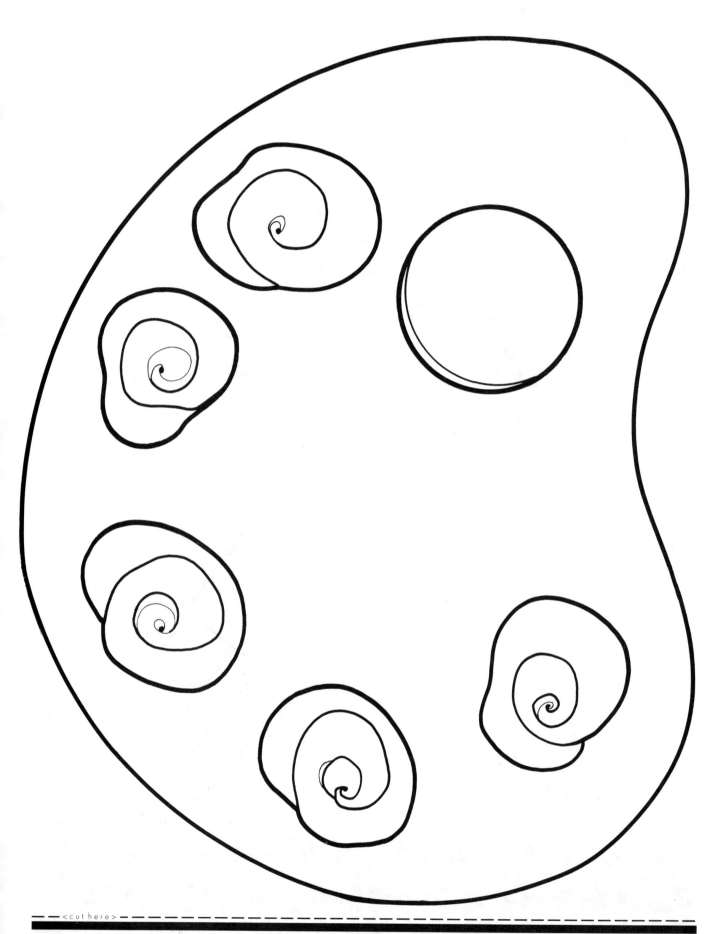

‒ ‒ ‒<cut here>‒ ‒

POSITIVE BEHAVIOR BULLETIN BOARD *See page 42 for instructions for use.*

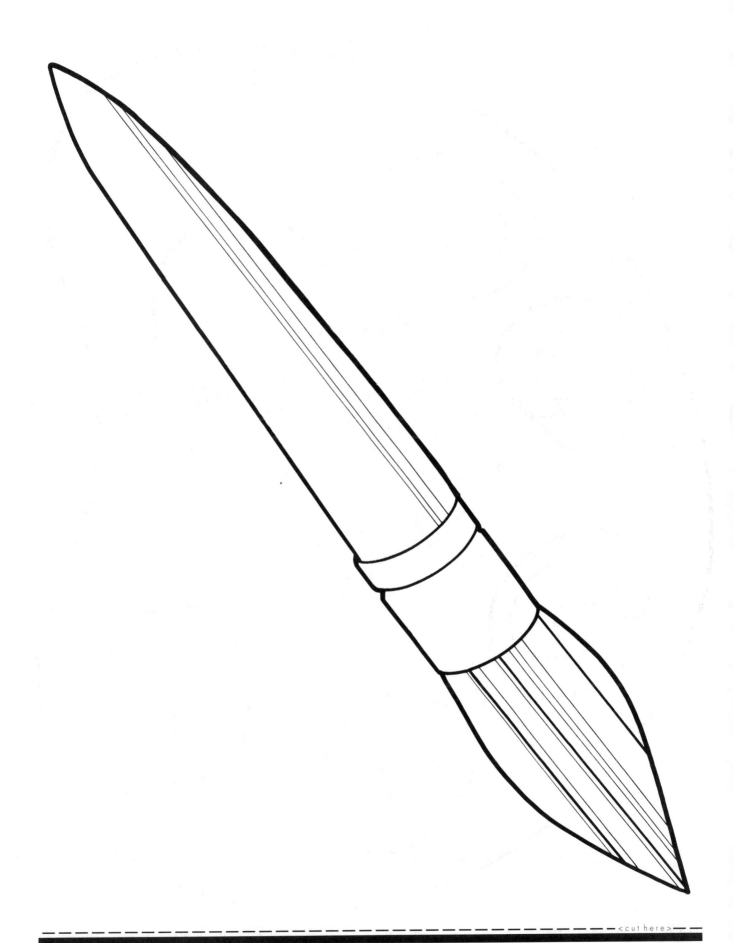

POSITIVE BEHAVIOR BULLETIN BOARD *See page 42 for instructions for use.*

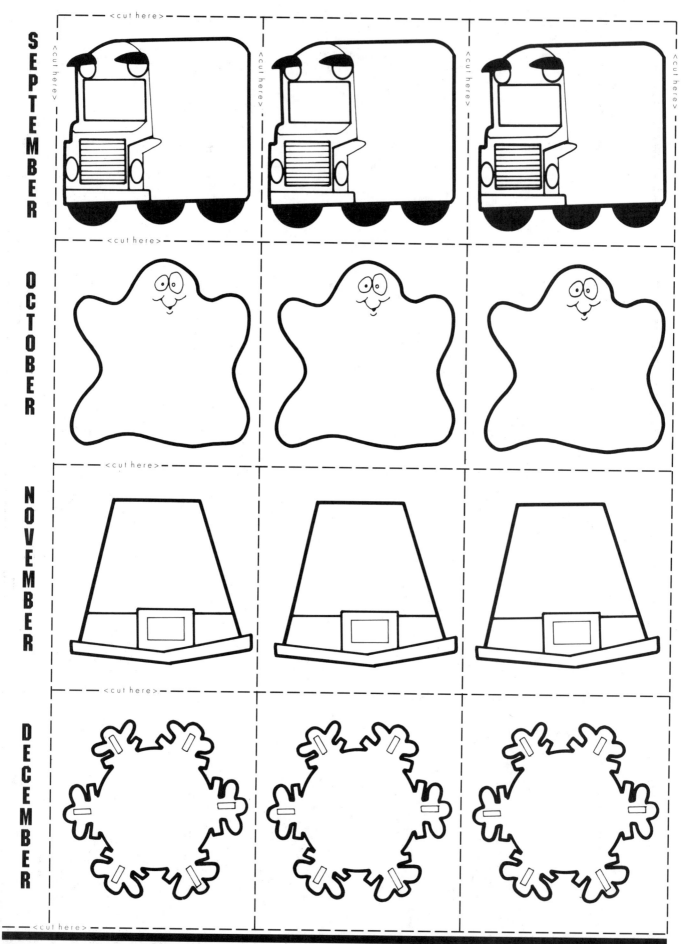

SEPTEMBER

OCTOBER

NOVEMBER

DECEMBER

CALENDAR DATE MARKERS *See page 45 for suggestions for use.*

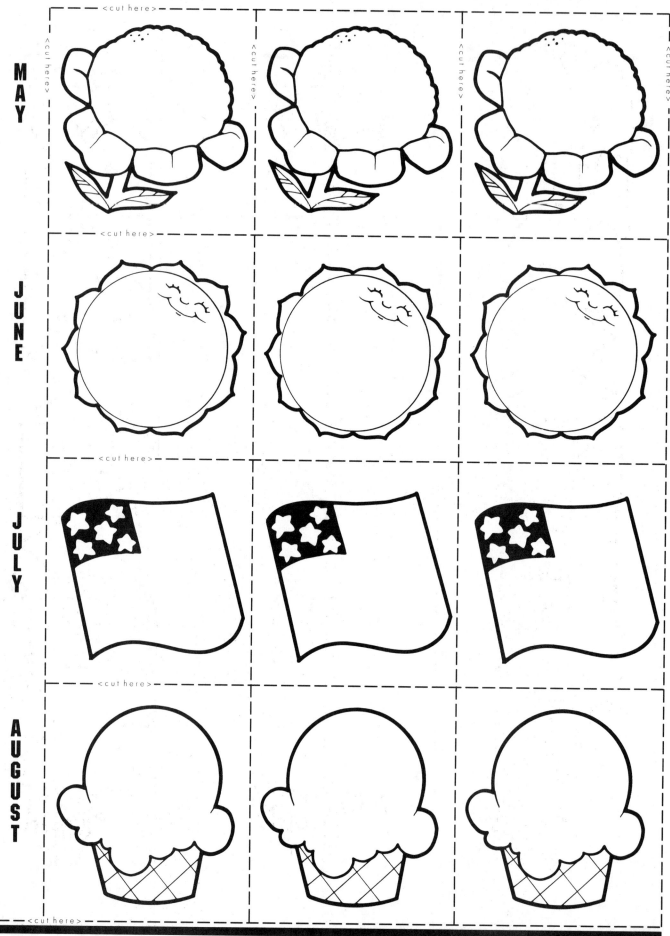

MAY

JUNE

JULY

AUGUST

CALENDAR DATE MARKERS *See page 45 for suggestions for use.*

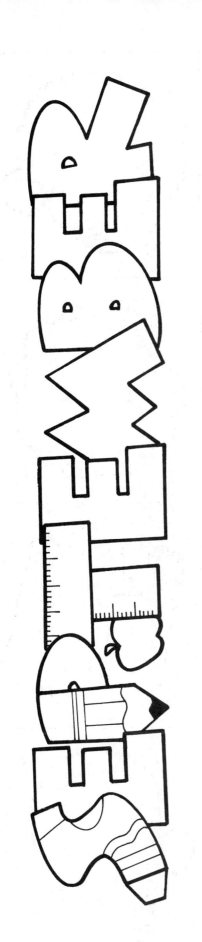

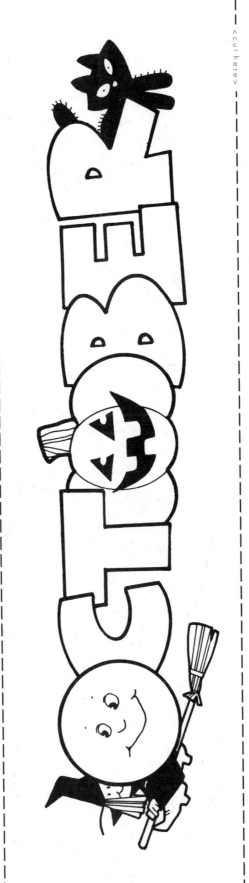

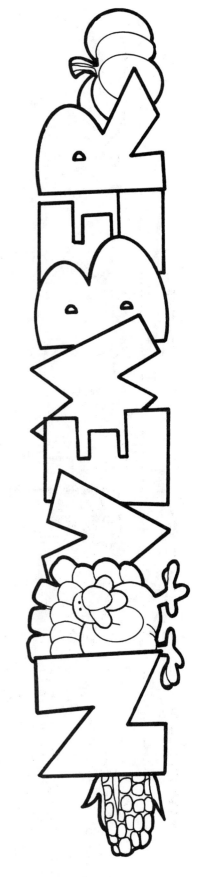

MONTHLY CALENDAR HEADLINERS *See page 45 for suggestions for use.*

—

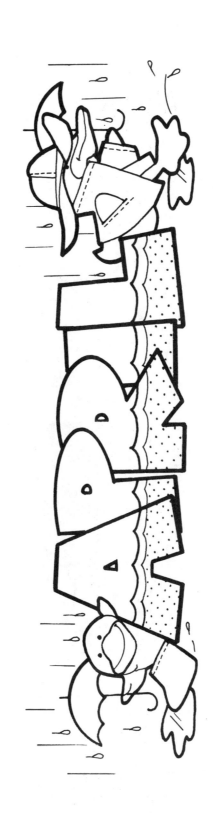

CLASS BIRTHDAY LIST!

Date

Name

CLASSROOM BIRTHDAY LIST *See page 46 for suggestions for use.*

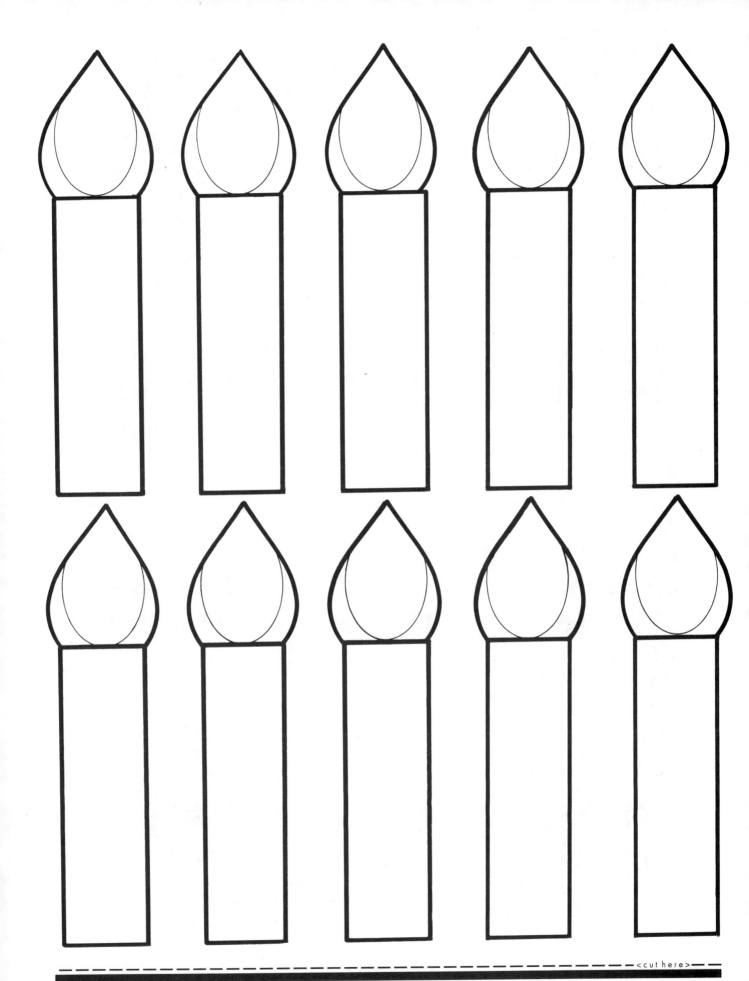

BULLETIN BOARD BIRTHDAY CANDLES   *See page 46 for suggestions for use.*

Line Leader

Paper Passer

Trash Controller

Chalk Monitor

Flag Salute Leader

Plant Patrol

Calendar Monitor

Class Go-Fer

Equipment Monitor

Closet Patrol

Window Person

Paper Carrier

   HELPERS CHART CARDS   *See page 46 for suggestions for use.*

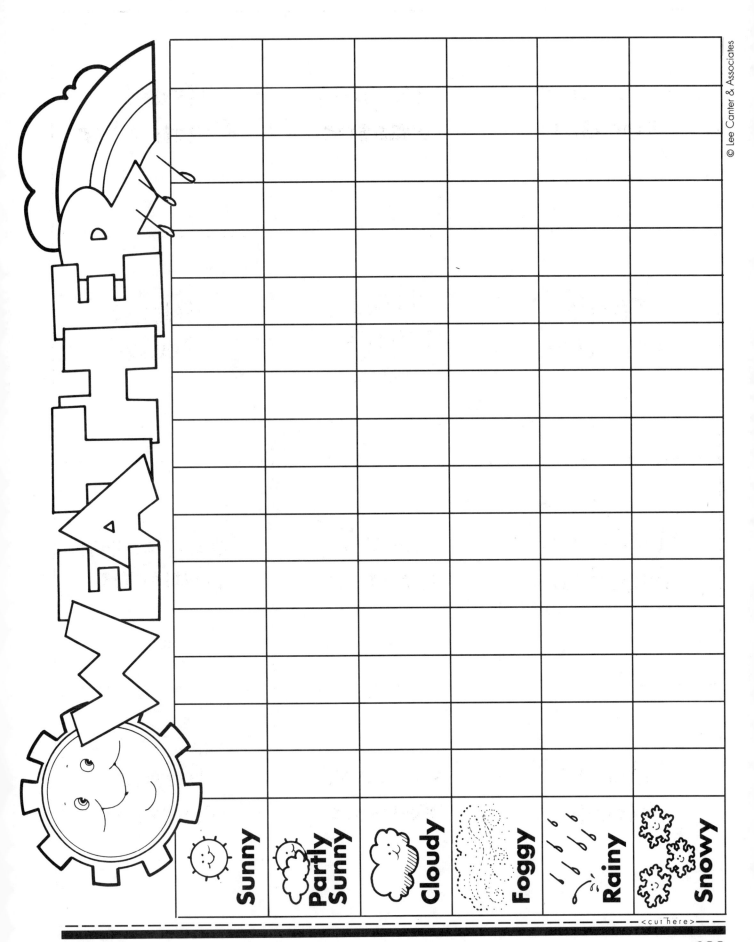

WEATHER

Sunny

Partly Sunny

Cloudy

Foggy

Rainy

Snowy

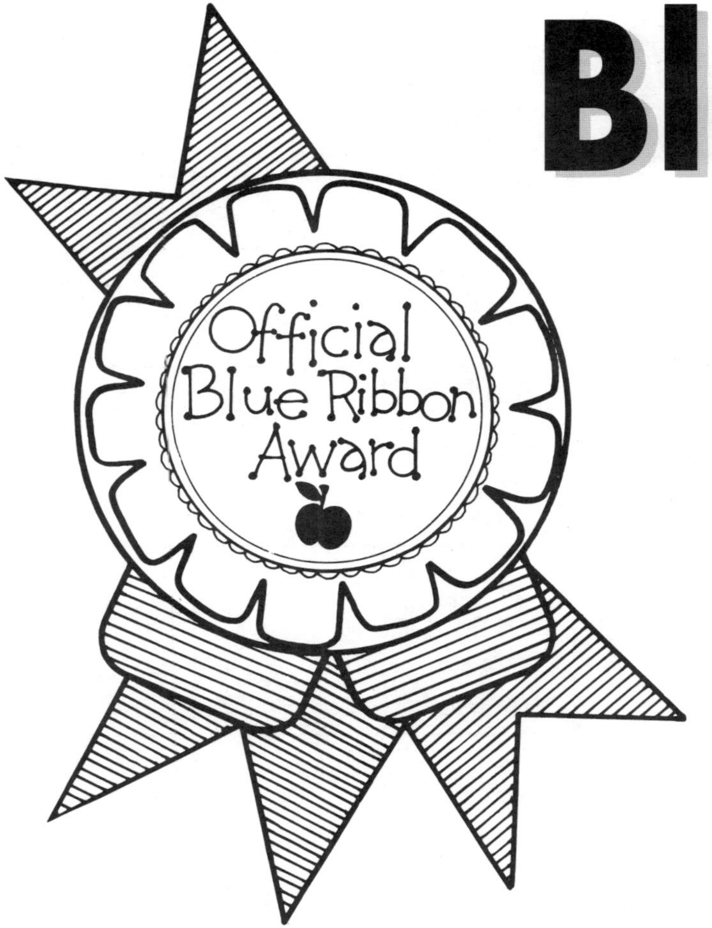

Blue Ribbon Certificate

Awarded to

_____

for

_____

Teacher's signature

_____

Date

Official Blue Ribbon Award

--- < c u t   h e r e > ---

	A	B	C	D	E	F
1						
2						
3						
4						
5						
6						
7						
8						

School is a "lotto" fun!

– – <cut here> –

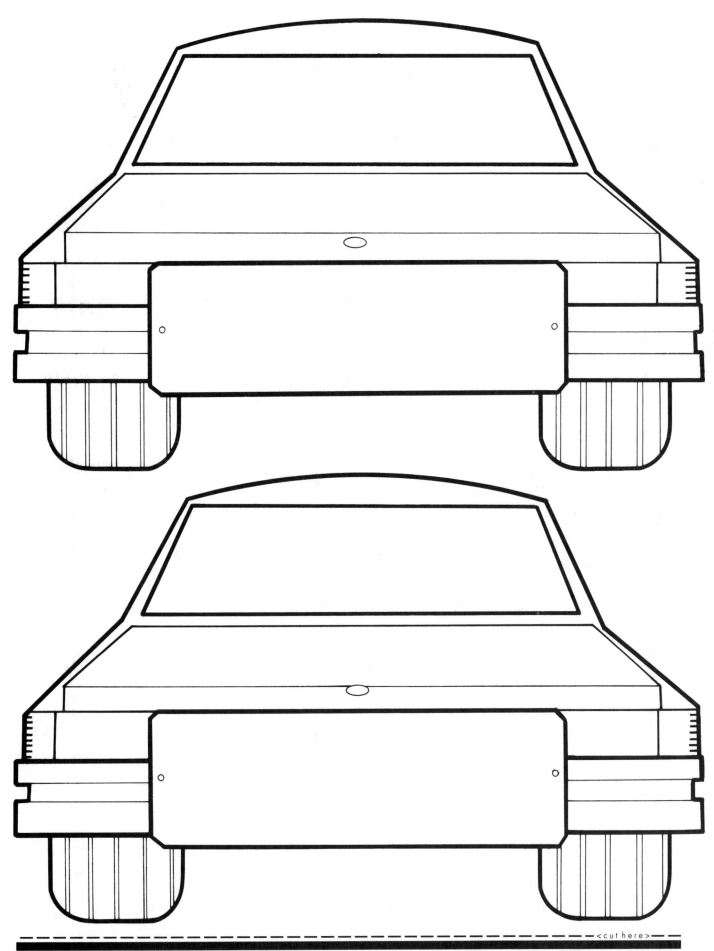

—<cut here>—

A-DOOR-ABLES *See page 48 for suggestions for use.*

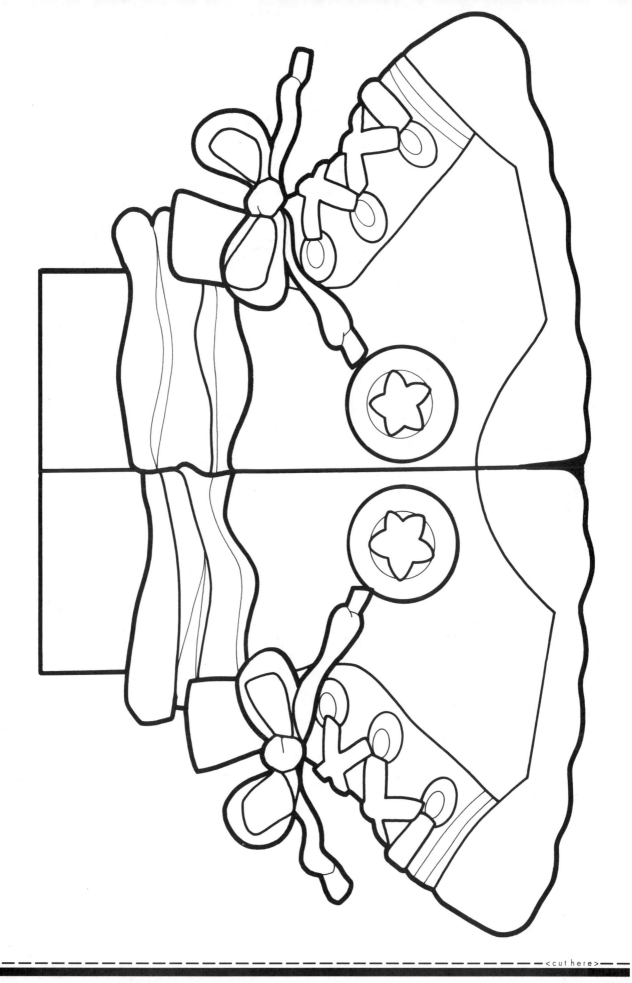

─ <cut here> ─

WELCOME

STUDENTS

Back-to-School
Parent Handbook

Teacher	Grade

Room Number

School

School Phone

School Year

You're invited to
Back-to-School Night.

_____

Place

_____

Date

_____

Time

Looking forward to seeing you,

_____

Teacher's signature

Thanks for attending!
Enter your child,

_____

in the Back-to-School Night raffle!

Thanks for attending!
Enter your child,

_____

in the Back-to-School Night raffle!

Thanks for attending!
Enter your child,

_____

in the Back-to-School Night raffle!

Thanks for attending!
Enter your child,

_____

in the Back-to-School Night raffle!

Thanks for attending!
Enter your child,

_____

in the Back-to-School Night raffle!

Thanks for attending!
Enter your child,

_____

in the Back-to-School Night raffle!

Thanks for attending!
Enter your child,

_____

in the Back-to-School Night raffle!

Thanks for attending!
Enter your child,

_____

in the Back-to-School Night raffle!

	A	B	C	D	E	F
1						
2						
3						
4						
5						
6						
7						
8						

Back to School Night Lotto

— <cut here> —

Looking Back at Back-to-School Night

Dear Parents:

— — — <cut here> —

Let's keep in touch! Use this form to write back with any questions or comments you may have.

To _____

_____

_____

_____

_____

_____

_____

From_____

— — <cut here> —

How to Help
Your Child
at Home

---- <cut here> ----

Dear Parent,
Our class could use an extra pair of hands.
We hope you can volunteer.
Here's what we need:

_____

_____

_____

_____

Signed _____ Date _____

☐ I'd be happy to help.
You can count on me to:

_____

_____

☐ Thank you for asking, but I will not
be able to help out this time.
Please ask me again.

Signed _____

CLASSROOM VOLUNTEER LETTER   *See page 58 for suggestions for use.*

Dear _____ ,

Thanks from the "bottom of my heart" for all your help. You're great!

Thanks,

— — — —< c u t h e r e >— —

Dear _____ ,

Thanks a "bunch" for all your help. I really appreciate it.

Thanks,

—< c u t h e r e >—

Working Together for Education

Call me if I can help:

_____

_____

TEACHING IS MY BUSINESS

Call me if I can help:

_____

_____

We Can Make the Difference

Call me if I can help:

_____

_____

The Path to Success
Let's work together...

Call me if I can help:

_____

_____

Working Together for Education

Call me if I can help:

_____

_____

TEACHING IS MY BUSINESS

Call me if I can help:

_____

_____

We Can Make the Difference

Call me if I can help:

_____

_____

The Path to Success
Let's work together...

Call me if I can help:

_____

_____

Teacher-Parent Telegram

To _____

_____

_____

_____

_____

_____

_____

_____

_____

Signed _____ **Date** _____

— — — <fold here> —

Reply

_____

_____

_____

_____

_____

_____

_____

_____

Signed _____ **Date** _____

— <cut here> — —

© Lee Canter & Associates

To the Parent(s) of _____

One of the keys to getting homework done is having supplies in one place. A Homework Survival Kit will prevent your child from continually being distracted by the need to go searching for supplies, and will free you from last-minute trips to the store for paper, tape, etc.

HOMEWORK SURVIVAL KIT

Checklist

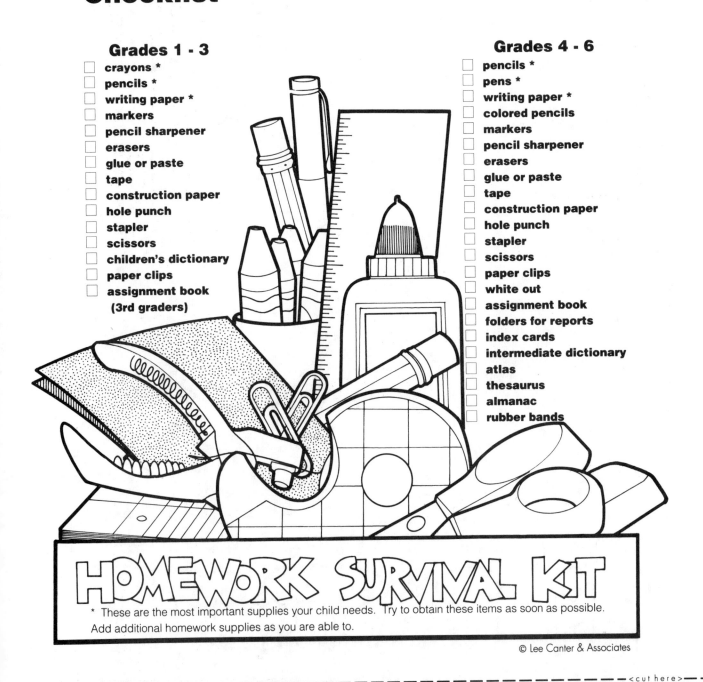

Grades 1 - 3
- ☐ crayons *
- ☐ pencils *
- ☐ writing paper *
- ☐ markers
- ☐ pencil sharpener
- ☐ erasers
- ☐ glue or paste
- ☐ tape
- ☐ construction paper
- ☐ hole punch
- ☐ stapler
- ☐ scissors
- ☐ children's dictionary
- ☐ paper clips
- ☐ assignment book
  (3rd graders)

Grades 4 - 6
- ☐ pencils *
- ☐ pens *
- ☐ writing paper *
- ☐ colored pencils
- ☐ markers
- ☐ pencil sharpener
- ☐ erasers
- ☐ glue or paste
- ☐ tape
- ☐ construction paper
- ☐ hole punch
- ☐ stapler
- ☐ scissors
- ☐ paper clips
- ☐ white out
- ☐ assignment book
- ☐ folders for reports
- ☐ index cards
- ☐ intermediate dictionary
- ☐ atlas
- ☐ thesaurus
- ☐ almanac
- ☐ rubber bands

HOMEWORK SURVIVAL KIT

* These are the most important supplies your child needs. Try to obtain these items as soon as possible. Add additional homework supplies as you are able to.

─────────────────────────────── —<cut here>—

HOMEWORK

DROP SPOT

—<cut here>—

HOMEWORK DROP SPOT SIGN *See page 69 for suggestions for use.*

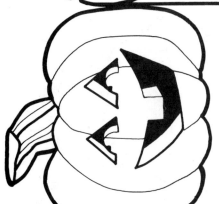

Student's name

You're real "**cool**" for doing a super job in school!

Student's name

Thanks for giving your best to each homework assignment.

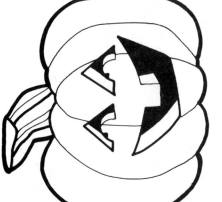

Student's name

Your good homework habits are "delightful." **Boo-tiful job!**

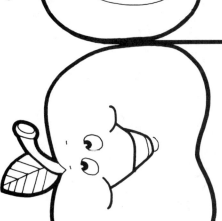

Student's name

Your good homework habits are very "appealing." **Thanks!**

SEASONAL HOMEWORK BOOKMARKS *See page 70 for suggestions for use.*

Student's name
_____

has the keys to good homework habits.

Signed _____ Date _____

Returning homework on time

Doing homework all by yourself

Doing your best job on your homework

© Lee Canter & Associates

— — — <cut here> — — — — — — — — — — — — — — — — —

Good homework habits are not extinct for

_____
Student's name

Signed _____ Date _____

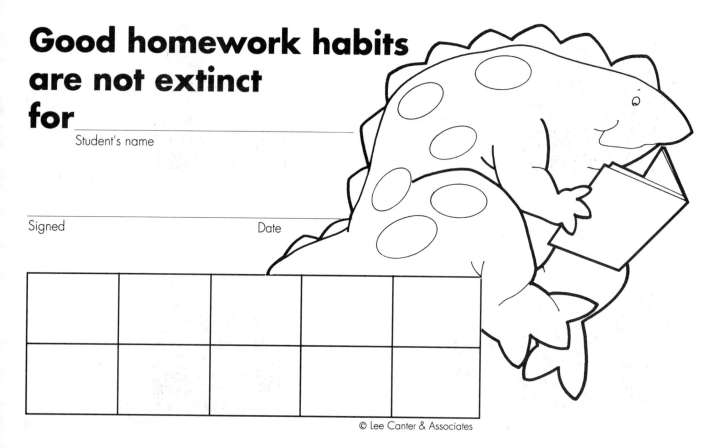

© Lee Canter & Associates

— — — <cut here> — — — — — — — — — — — —

HOMEWORK MOTIVATOR AWARDS   *See page 70 for suggestions for use.*

 **1st in Line**
Homework Habits

 **15 Minutes Free Time**
Homework Habits

 **Teacher's Assistant**
Homework Habits

 **15 Minutes Reading Time**
Homework Habits

 **Messenger for a Day**
Homework Habits

 _____
Homework Habits

 **Sit at Teacher's Desk**
Homework Habits

 _____
Homework Habits

See page 70 for suggestions for use.

GOOD HOMEWORK HABITS POSTER *See page 71 for suggestions for use.*

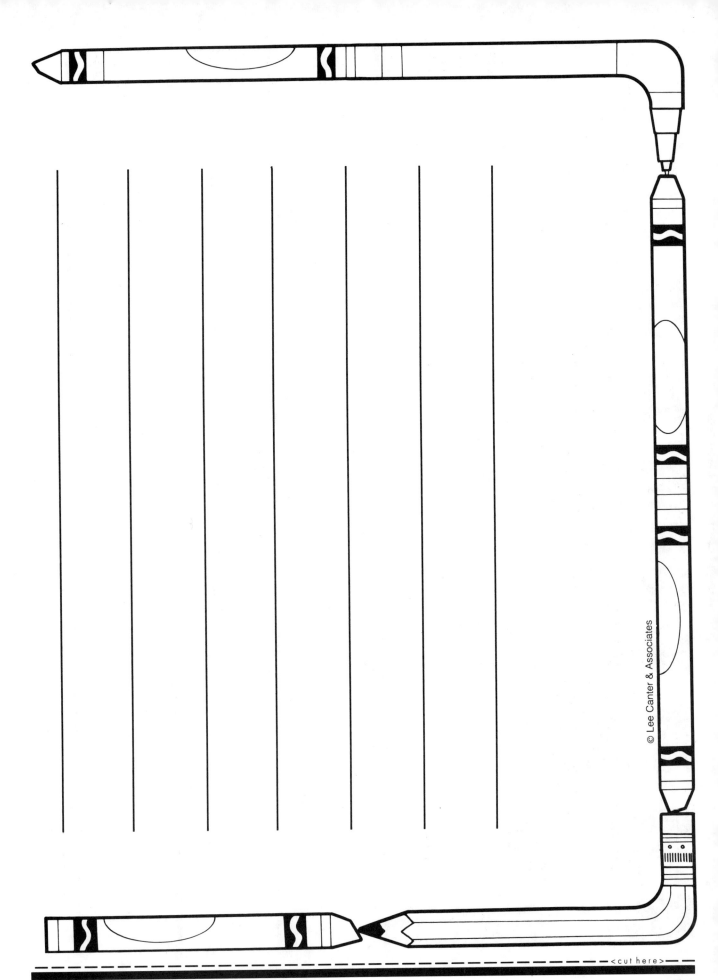

© Lee Canter & Associates

HOMEWORK

FOR

Assignment Date

HOMEWORK CHART   *See page 71 for suggestions for use.*

Homework Sheet

Name _____

Week of _____

Spelling Words

M				
T				
W				
TH				
F				

P.S. _____
Parent Signature

BACK-TO-SCHOOL NAME VISOR

Run off copies of the Back-to-School Name Visor on sturdy paper. Give to students to cut and color.

1. Write your name on the visor.
2. Cut it out.
3. Tie string through each hole.
4. Wear your new visor!

Punch holes with hole punch.

Name

Things I wish I had done this summer:

Things I'm glad I didn't do this summer:

BINGO

			☆ Free	
☆ Free				
		☆ Free		
				☆ Free
	☆ Free			

© Lee Canter & Associates

MAGIC SQUARE

What makes this square magic? Many things are hiding in the Magic Square and you can be the one to find them! Just follow the directions and you will find a dog and a house.

1 Cut the Magic Square apart along the lines.
2 Place the Magic Square pieces on the table.
3 Arrange the pieces in any order until you have made a dog or a house.

Here is what the dog and the house look like. Now, what other pictures can you make with the Magic Squares?

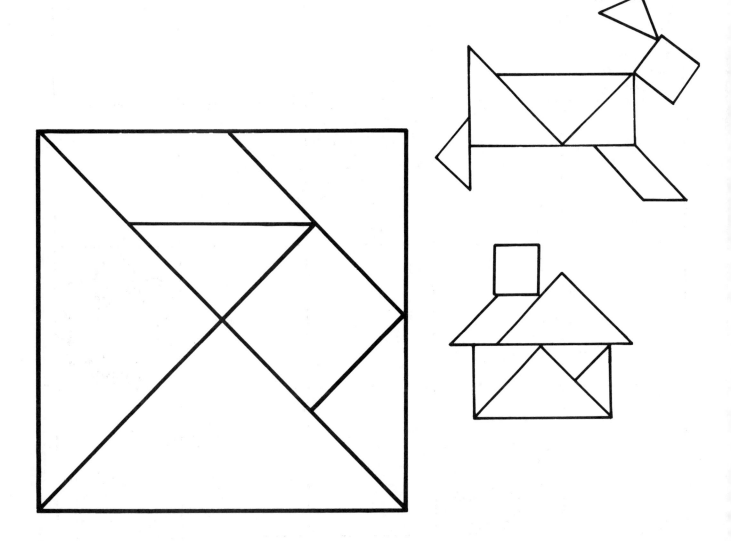

MONDAY	TUESDAY	WEDNESDAY	THURSDAY	FRIDAY

OPEN-ENDED CALENDAR *See page 76 for suggestions for use.*

ALL ABOUT ME

My name is _____

This is a picture of me.

------- <cut here> ------------------------------

This is my family.

ALL ABOUT ME

Their names are

_____

ALL ABOUT ME

This is where I live.

My address is

_____

- - - <cut here> -

ALL ABOUT ME

This is my friend.
We are friends
because

_____

_____

_____

_____

- - <cut here> -

These are my favorites:

ALL ABOUT ME

color

animal

food

TV show

game

holiday

- - - <cut here> -

When I grow up, I would like to

ALL ABOUT ME

_____

- - - <cut here> - -

< fold here >

sı ǝɯɐu ʎW

< fold here >

My name is

< fold here >

3-D DESK TAGS *See page 78 for suggestions for use.*

Daily Schedule

Time	Monday	Tuesday	Wednesday	Thursday	Friday
8:00					
8:30					
9:00					
9:30					
10:00					
10:30					
11:00					
11:30					
12:00					
12:30					
1:00					
1:30					
2:00					
2:30					
3:00					
3:30					

_____

_____

_____

When I choose not to follow the rules: _____

_____

_____

_____

<fold here>

When I follow the rules: _____

_____

_____

_____

_____

_____

_____

_____

These are the rules for our classroom: _____

— <fold here> —

Parent: Read and discuss this booklet with your child.

I have read and understood the rules and consequences.

_____
Student's name

_____
Parent signature   Date

My Building
GOOD BEHAVIOR
Booklet

SPIKE

— <cut here> —

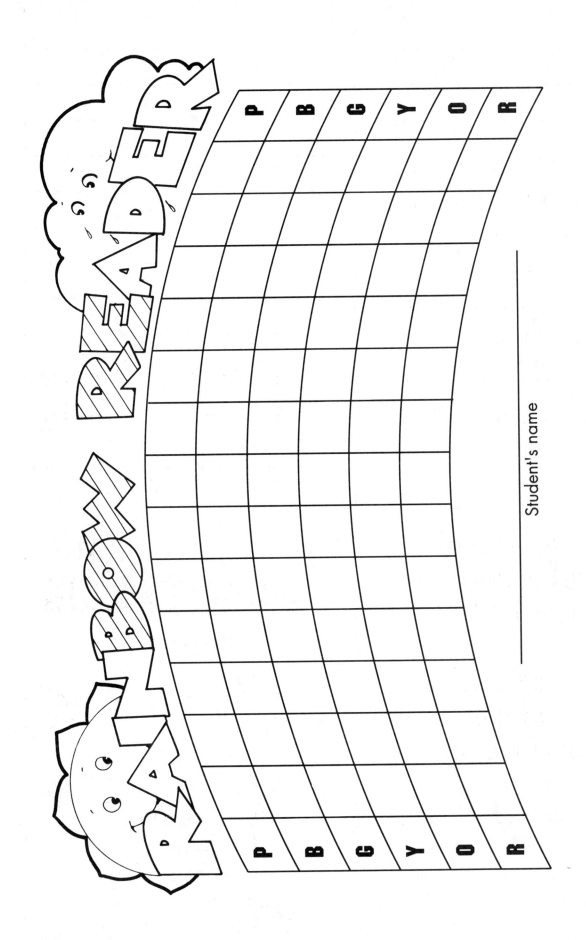

Student's name

SOMETHING IS "BUGGING" ME NOTES   *See page 91 for suggestions for use.*